Sit Your Self Down

Gayatri Jayaraman is a counsellor and has been a journalist in the Indian media for over 20 years. She set up Shamah | शमः, a mind-body-spirit practice in Mumbai.

PRAISE FOR THE BOOK

'One can spend a lifetime, or many lifetimes, studying and practising the Dharmic way. It is deep, ethereal, and brings the soul home. Vipassana is one of the many paths within the Dharmic way. The most important thing in a journey is the first step. Gayatri, a thinker with deep intellect, and yet adept at simple, easy words, is one of the best companions for that first step. Read this very easy-to-read yet deeply insightful book and begin your journey.' – Amish, author

'I have found vipassana immensely beneficial. It made me realize I need to focus on my strengths and give my best. Gayatri's experiences in this book will inspire readers and give them an insider's view of this transformative experience.' – Anu Aga, business leader and philanthropist

First published in 2020 by Hachette India
(Registered name: Hachette Book Publishing India Pvt. Ltd)
An Hachette UK company
www.hachetteindia.com

SRD

ISBN 978-93-89253-55-9

Hachette Book Publishing India Pvt. Ltd
4th/5th Floors, Corporate Centre,
Plot No. 94, Sector 44, Gurugram 122003, India

Typeset in Arno Pro 12/15.9
by Manmohan Kumar, Delhi

Printed and bound in India by Manipal Technologies Limited, Manipal

FSC
www.fsc.org
MIX
Paper from responsible sources
FSC™ C104740

Sit Your Self Down

A Novice's Journey into the Heart of Vipassana

Gayatri Jayaraman

hachette
INDIA

Ye ca sangha atītā ca
Ye ca sangha anāgatā
Paccupannā ca ye sangha
Ahaṃvandāmi sabbadā

To the sanghas of the past
To the sanghas of the future
To the sangha of the present
My respect, always

Sandhiṭṭiko
To be seen for oneself
Akāliko
To obtain results in the now
Ehi-passiko
To invite others to come and see
Opaneyyiko
To lead to the goal

Contents

Author's Note

THE EXPERIENCES DISCUSSED IN THIS BOOK ARE indicative of my personal practice only and should not be considered a replacement for actual teaching. Vipassana can only be learnt by initiation via an assistant teacher at authorized centres worldwide. I followed the course at a centre of the Vipassana Institute, Dhammagiri, Igatpuri, India.

The Pali and Hindi suttas and chants in this book have been cited from *The Gem Set in Gold*, published by the Vipassana Research Institute, Igatpuri, in 2006. Discourses cited are from *The Discourse Summaries*, condensed by William Hart, published by the Vipassana Research Institute, Igatpuri, in 1996.

The names of all other participants in the course have been changed to protect their privacy.

Day 0

Steep, Sleep, Seep

I STEP OFF THE JOLTING JALOPY OF A SHARED-SEAT jeep taxi into a dead end on the ridge, and it takes me a minute to realize that here on in there is no road at all. There is only a climb. I am standing at the base of what must surely be a hundred steps leading up into the foliage that fronts the meditation centre. The Assam Lingzey Ridge has been chiselled by the bluster that the unforgiving Kanchenjunga periodically sends its way. I am a minuscule climber, an ant in the mulch beneath a leaf fallen from a tree trembling in the face of the winds lashing it, and I evoke little even by way of pathos from its stony rock face. I feel a twinge of regret – I should have carried my backpack, like I had first planned to, before I switched to a suitcase. Before I wondered if it would be colder than I imagined and added some more clothes. More layers. More changes. More just-in-cases to the suitcase I must now brace an incline with. Some people seem to have reached the top already, partially obscured by the leafy curtain. They are looking down and wondering if I need help. Right now, it feels like all the world can see my folly. This is my climb to climb alone. I consider leaving, calling back the jeep driver who overcharged me, more than double what the locals pay, to leave me here. It is just a momentary thought that I bury in its grave immediately

– from where it will resurrect several times over the next few days. I ought to have cremated it instead. But even that results in rebirth, I am to learn. There is no escape from thoughts I would rather not think. It's now or never. I waited for the son to grow up so I could leave him unsupervised. He will be off to college soon, leaving me the dog to watch over. This window of time is all I have. I am relieved they haven't asked us to justify why we have come and why here. My answers would have been quite ambiguous. I need something that dissolves me, my past and future, into a seamless route, so I can see where I am going. I can't say for sure I'll find my answers here, but I'll try anything once. I brace to take four steps at a time, then rest, then begin again. By step 16, I hope there is a better way. What is it they say about winding temple steps? That the arduous path is part of the process... this is some Mr Miyagi training built into the access road. As I near the summit, someone finally asks if I need help with my bag, but it's come too late. The steps run closer together now, in a hurry to ascend. So am I.

'I tried to call you, but you didn't pick up,' the office administrator complains as I reach the final step. I had long stopped counting – after step 64. My breath is emerging in visible puffs now. I hustle a grumble.

'I was tackling your stairs. It was one or the other,' I gasp.

He laughs good-naturedly. He has heard it before. I reach for my phone to check my missed calls. If my only take-home from this trip is holding this slavish habit in check, I am willing to count it a win. I message home that I have reached, and the administrator watches as I switch my phone off.

'No reading material, I hope?'

'Only my airline ticket,' I say.

'I'll take that,' he retorts, 'or you will be contemplating your departure throughout.'

Incredulous, I hand it over and watch it disappear into a cloth bag. He lets me keep my cherry-red alarm clock, though it seems larger, brighter and potentially louder here than it did at home. He seems disapproving.

'Don't let it ring. You can use it to check the time in the mornings. In the day, you won't need it.'

Who doesn't need the time of day?

'I can't help you carry your bag to your room because I have thrown out my back,' he adds.

By now that is the least of my worries. I follow him up the stairs to the area marked 'Female' – the men have their own entrances, exits and dwellings that we are not privy to, but I suspect, snarkily to myself, they have the better view of the valley and the mountains beyond. Ours is a back-to-front cottage, its mouth to a stone wall, its shoulders to the riverine valley beyond. What a waste of a view, I think. This is a small centre. There are only dormitories open to us here. It is not yet 6 p.m. and it is already dark this far east. It is too late to turn back now, and not just for want of light. I can do this.

They allot me a bed, the third of four in a room, each cordoned off from the others by ringed blue curtains, like in a hospital ward. I consider throwing a fuss and asking for a single room, but choose to think of college, roomies and revolution instead.

Every fibre of my mind is already signalling rebellion, straining like a dog unused to being leashed – a spoilt pet. Just as the panic rises, I hear the voices of other women. Shy hellos. More trickle in. A cheerful sevika walks in and hands us our bedding. Her name is Dechen. She is an experienced hand, a senior, whom we are allowed to speak to when we need help. Her presence is a solace. Two of our batch are late, caught in the dark creeping rapidly up the hillside, and we worry if they'll reach before the orientation programme. We leave our belongings, make our beds and huddle on the porch, sipping hot water from a dispenser, each pretending that it is somewhat stronger a salve.

Jessica is in her mid-twenties and has been travelling around the world from home in Toronto for a year now. She's worked numerous short stints, more recently in the forest department as a ranger. She was in Darjeeling when she saw a notice for the course. Statuesque Diana from Vancouver is in her fifties, travelling through South East Asia. Srijana is from Gangtok, and points to the twinkling lights in approximation of her home. Raima is from Kalimpong, and Sita is from Pakyong, near the new airport, which is

10 kilometres away from where we are. Raima and Sita are the same height, and already seem like sisters. Neena, a former government employee, is a soft-spoken artist from Aurangabad, halfway down the country. An elderly woman whom we later come to know as Mrs Pradhan only speaks Bangla, so she wraps herself in a shawl and listens to the English and Hindi banter, saying nothing. Her son, a government employee, is in the male quarters at the other end of the property. I wonder if he brought her or she him. She carries herself in quiet resignation.

The dark is rapidly creeping up the hillside now, and we wait with some trepidation for the missing two, who are sending us periodic updates on the WhatsApp group that the sevika still has access to. Already, we all feel inextricably tied into a deepening bond with each other – we who don't know what to expect from this and from ourselves, let alone from each other, but are here anyway. We go around asking ourselves, more than each other, why we are here. I want to say that I miss the sensation of my laughter, rising from my middle, like a gurgling spring of unconfined joy. I want to remove what feels like a force field against tears inside me now. Instead, I hear myself tell them that I waited fifteen years to come here because I could not leave my son alone without being able to contact him even in an emergency for the entire ten-day duration. He will be eighteen soon and leaving home for college in a few months, and I feel like I'm standing on the threshold of a new phase of my own life – me as just me, as opposed to me as a mother. The truth is several layers deeper. I am all that he has had. I am finally here, even if his disappointment with my decision comes as a surprise. To him it seems personal – for me to cut myself off from him so completely. He doesn't understand it. When he and I, mother and child, have shared everything, what was it that I needed to do now that he couldn't be a part of? For once, I couldn't explain, and I couldn't include him either. I have come here to cry the tears I have never allowed him to see. I get to do that alone now. All I'm saying is it's empty nest syndrome. I shrug and smile at the group. They get what is unsaid as much as what is. Srijana thought she wanted to be a chartered accountant and has ended up in marketing, but doesn't know where she would rather be – all she knows is it is elsewhere. We think of Jessica as soaking in the India experience, a flighty trip, but I sense that she is fragile. Diana would like to use her hands to heal. Raima and Sita don't say anything. They offer no reason for being here and that seems to suffice. Our reasons are veiled, but our minds are open to the process, or at least we think they are. I wonder in what ways we have each been hurt that we are here now, knowing the answers are no longer outside of us.

The gong sounds through the air – the last supper as it were. From tomorrow, once the course starts, we will have no meal after the evening tea, and no real food after lunch.

When the steaming rice and the bounteous fresh mountain vegetables and dals are laid out, we eat a little more than we each mean to. As we finish, the missing two appear. Navya is a cardiologist from Coimbatore, and Ana is a marine engineer from Trichy, both in their mid-twenties and hailing from the deep south. Ana will for many months be the only woman on the ship she navigates and is the only one in the group who has done this before, doing a course each time she sets sail. There is barely time to catch up as they are allotted their beds, and we are ushered into the orientation room, plastic chairs in the space we just ate dinner in, for the first session.

The office administrator reappears. He is grimmer now and bows to the television set on which a pre-recorded message will shortly play the rules of the stay. I make a mental note to never be the kind of person who bows to television sets. 'If you are tempted to leave, the time is now,' the office administrator says. 'Once you begin the course, it will not only be disallowed, it could also be harmful to stop a course of learning halfway.' Nobody volunteers, but you could slather a slice of bread with the tension in the room and eat it for tea. We're adults, we can do this, we're all telling ourselves. I half-expect Diana, sitting behind me such that I cannot see her face without pointedly turning around, to ask to leave, as she didn't seem to like the living quarters. The moment passes. If we stay, we must ask to receive the teaching of anāpānasati, referred to simply as 'ana-pana' by the teachers, the first stage of meditation, TV Bowman insists. We follow the chants on the recording to make a formal request.

> Nibannassa sachikaranatthaya me bhante ana-pana kammathannam dehi.
>
> For the sake of witnessing nirvana, sir, grant me the meditation object of ana-pana.

You may have travelled halfway around the world and physically checked into a meditation centre, but till you formally request the learning, you cannot be initiated. My journalist brain cranks into sharp response mode. The world I have just left behind has been bemoaning the lack of insight that men have about the need for female consent. All along, here, hidden away in caves, monasteries and meditation centres, groups of monks have been quietly practising the art of consent for centuries. Perhaps the government ought to simply incorporate this practice of asking for a student's consent, right from the school level, expanding it to other relationships in life, to drive the lesson home.

The chants now finished, we are instructed into Noble Silence and, for the duration of the course, may not gesture or communicate in any way, not so much as even catch our neighbour's eye, so my thoughts on how to transform male behaviour must remain confined to myself a while longer.

~

The schedule that we are to follow for the next ten days is up on a noticeboard outside the women's living quarters. The day begins at 4 a.m., we meditate till 6.30 a.m., break for breakfast, resume at 8 a.m. and go on till 11 a.m., lunch till 1 p.m., meditate till 5 p.m. in two sessions, break for tea until 6.30 p.m., meditate till 7.30 p.m. and then watch a video of the teacher's discourse before a quick half hour of meditation, and then bed. Well, at least it's not the Hunger Games. My son was worried it might be. It sounds exhausting nevertheless. So much nothing to do for so many hours. I hope one of us doesn't lose it halfway through.

Day 1

Meet Monkey Mind

I AM AN EARLY RISER INASMUCH AS ANY DOG OWNER is – my alarm clock the overenthusiastic tongue of a hyperactive pet promised a walk at 6 a.m. and bounding about in preparatory mode a whole half hour earlier. Even so, I would not describe my pre-dawn thought process as meditative until maybe up to a whole hour later. That is a state of mind that descends with the morning cuppa, crisp with ginger and bracing with sugar, perhaps with a Raag Jog playing to lift me gently out of my somnolence. You see, then, that the first gong at 4 a.m., followed by fairy bells chiming through the crisp air, does not bring you into that state of alertness the organizers must have hoped it would. You would think that thrusting one's fingers into icy tap waters to wash up would shock you awake, but I found the effect to be the opposite – kind of like prodding a dozing turtle sharply such that it withdraws into its shell. Everything is slower even as I will my body to move faster. I retreat under my shawl. Some bring their entire double-layered sleeping blankets. You travel with your whole house to the meditation hall by the 4.30 gong, as though it has taken you quite a few lifetimes to actually get there. Thankfully, no one is talking; there is no guidance at this stage and you can peacefully spend the whole morning hour inserting each folded leg into the other's gap, the pretzel contortions of the ardhapadmasana, from where they will repeatedly escape like a pair of caged animals seeking to reclaim their primal states. My body, and from what I could tell through the grogginess, those of others, responds by tilting like a collapsing cake.

The hour done, the morning chants in Pali begin. Day 1 is the Āṭānāṭiya Sutta. The passages from the Dīgha-nikāya III.9 and the last one from the Dhammapada VIII.10 pay homage to the seven buddhas, or enlightened ones, who came before Siddhartha, who became Gautama, the Buddha. The incomprehensible chants in the voice of the teacher spread through the hall, a thin sliver of the land of the awake for the inevitably sleeping. Consciousness, this way.

It is only at the breakfast queue that I notice Diana. She is weeping copiously, her face a ripened plum. She shovels some chickpeas in tomato gravy and some grainy porridge onto her plate with distaste, and I assume the food, though not spicy, is unsuitable to the needs of those unused to it. It is not, after all, staple breakfast fare. I want to go up to her and commiserate, or console, but we are in Noble Silence. I am not supposed to have noticed that she is in tears. I notice we are all doing the same, noticing that we are not supposed to be noticing that we are each noticing. Looking at her and looking away, unable to communicate, and eating uncomfortably. There is something unnatural about not being able to reach out, to be buried so deeply within one's own mind that the discomfort of another ceases to bother you. I am grateful we are not there yet. It would be disappointing to find oneself unmoved. Dechen, who is serving food, steps in. Dechen and Diana are now in conversation, and we focus on our food, relieved that the problem is in all probability being solved.

I sprint to grab an empty bathroom. We may use the post-meal hours to bathe, drawing water from one of three geysers outside the common bathrooms and taking a half-bucketful in. The bathroom roofs are simple asbestos sheets raised over coarse cement blocks, and the cold air gusts in through the gaps. I shiver as I bathe, but the alternating cold and heat shakes me out of the daze of the morning. My bones feel resolved, and the ache in my shins from the climb of the previous day has vanished. I vow to do this every morning, no matter the weather. We have not been allowed to bring deodorants here because they disturb meditation and I do not want to be the one raising a stink.

Post breakfast, with some tea in us, refreshed, one is better equipped to tackle the practice. Ana-pana begins. The meditation itself is simple, an age-old technique that, if you're Indian or follow any form of yoga, you've probably been taught several times over from childhood. Just focus your mind on your breath – as it goes in and as it comes out. You are not to chant any mantra or visualize any gods while you do this. Chanting mantras or visualizing gods makes it more difficult to focus, especially if you are used to it. These techniques bring your mind to focus more quickly, but they keep the mind on the shell – the visualization acts as a placebo, giving you the false joy of focus, when it is, in fact, obstructing the harder work of mastering the mind and exploring the depths of reality. It detracts from the deeper, abstract meditation that you are capable of as you advance. This is like giving a child a pacifier until their mealtime. They have something to focus on that keeps them from thrashing about and we mistake their lack of thrashing about as peace, as an assuaging of hunger. Yogic breathing techniques also focus on the intentional breaths, via pranayam or anulom vilom. These are regulated breaths, hitting the depths within and drawn deeply out. Neither of those techniques are used here. This is simple observation of the normal breath. Observe it go in and go out. If it's short, let it be short. If it's long, let it be long. Follow what is, observe what is. Don't mess with it. Don't regulate it. Don't alter it. Just notice it. It sounds simple enough.

Great. All I have to do now is ignore the coughing and rustling of my fellow meditators, the trilling of the birds, the drone of the Siliguri–Gangtok helicopter service somewhere above, flying tourists to their hotels or possibly politicians back and forth, which means the weather must be clear today, elections imminent, and somewhere I can hear a buzz saw begin...the way these people chop down trees in the hills – all the scenic wonderlands are tourist traps turning into concrete jungles now! – somewhere school children are noisily on their way...and I finally return to my breath, three-quarters of an hour later, having wandered virtually through Sikkim and the recesses of my mind. Turns out, the tip of one's nostrils are not fascinating enough to grab my attention for hours together. Who knew? The morning hours are up, and enlightenment seems to have hopped on a bus and moved one stop further down the trail.

Breathe

Lunch is steaming-hot white mountain rice and fresh vegetables, a simple cholar dal and rotis. There are three kinds of vegetables: simple village greens, gourds and a third mix, all light, fresh and non-spicy. There's a paneer chutney, made by grinding red chillies, a garlic pod and cottage cheese. Slices of fresh, tender white radish fleck the paste. It's irresistible. And freshly cut cucumbers, carrots and tomatoes. It's a reminder of those simple home-cooked meals that I've stopped taking the effort to make every day. I resolve to cook more earnestly and order in less when I return. We are each allotted a plate, a bowl, cutlery and a napkin at an assigned seat, and we must wash our utensils and replace them before we exit. Everything is done in perfect silence, from queueing up for the meal to the line at the wash facility. The only communication we have is from the sevika who asks us how we are doing, explains the food options, or simply smiles. We each hang on to her, unaccustomed to this well of silence, like she's the rope on the pulley that will fish us out of here one day. She must need to be so strong as to carry that burden, or she will fray, I can't help thinking. We are two to a table and at mine is one of my roommates. She insists on looking at me and smiling, or gesturing to ask me if I want seconds as she goes to the table to help herself, and it irritates me. It feels like an unwelcome intrusion into my self-appointed cloistering. Doesn't she know the rules? She doesn't take it seriously, I have decided. I am superior to her because I take this, my spiritual growth, seriously. In another world, she would have just been being nice. But we are not in another world now. We are in a world where nice is an intrusion too.

I return to the room, hoping to catch a snooze before the afternoon session. Diana's things in her bed next to me are packed. Ah! She is leaving, I think sadly. It's a pity – she would have benefited from the course. We Indians are far more rigorous than the West is, more used to passable sanitation facilities, less privacy and more cohabitation. She probably came here thinking it would be a fad goat yoga weekend in a luxury spa retreat, something to Instagram later, perhaps. But why is the woman on the far right also packing? Wait, what? Apparently, Diana hasn't had a night's sleep. Sita neither. Both have requested to move to a shared spare room below. I heard some snoring, I imagine, but I have seasoned ears and sounds float through my consciousness as I drift away. The cardiologist, it must be. She returns to the room, draws up her blankets, shuts the door and is lost to oblivion. She does not notice that both Diana and Sita have moved out, and we are left, the two of us potential snorers, marked women. Some people are just so insensitive, I think, as the pending sleep of the pre-dawn shift consumes me.

I spend much of the post-noon sessions contemplating the potential of my culpability in disturbing the night's peace. How terrible for people to have come here for silence and be disturbed by raucous snoring. I have no way of asking if it was me. I am not supposed to get involved in someone else's business. I am here to focus on my own. It would be gossipy and inappropriate, prying of me even, to go to the sevika and ask why the women shifted. I can therefore only assume. The supposed snoring, that nobody has accused anybody of or blamed anyone for, has taken on epic proportions in my head. In my mind, it filters down the hillside and into the valley beyond, echoing through the hills, the progenitor locked in involuntary stupor, keeping the townsfolk awake and in agony. If it was indeed me, it would mean I have snored so loudly that

I made a grown woman cry. I nurse a sense of being wounded. I nurture my ego as the blamed but helpless one. I suddenly think of what my son would say. Undoubtedly, he would love this. I can visualize him going off into peals of laughter, and I giggle. I open my eyes to see if anyone has noticed. The assistant teacher, an elderly Bengali gentleman wrapped in three different shawls and a monkey cap, who watches us like a hawk, is looking at the men's side right now. I feel lighter instantly. Okay, so maybe I snore. That's one more thing I have learnt about myself in a day and it's not like I can do anything about it if I do. I am here to solve the things about myself that I can. Worst case, without dinner I will end the ten days having lost some weight hopefully, so it won't be a complete waste. And this should teach me to be so smug. No one likes a self-righteous spiritualist. Only one rung below the self-righteous fitness freak. I shrug and close my eyes again. I formulate a new motto for myself: 'What I can do, I will do. What I can't, well, I can't.' I have reached the age where I am unable to apologize for myself any more. I am flawed, but I am here to embrace my flaws. The mind continues to wander, but it returns quicker. At the very least, I can tell when I am wandering off again. Not being invested in any specific outcome helps. Perhaps that is the germ of awareness.

I take an extra cuppa at tea. It is weak and has no ginger like I am used to, but my fingers are just grateful to even have a warm tumbler to hug. It is so cold you can feel the path the hot liquid traces as it makes its way down your gullet. The norm is a bowl of muri (puffed rice seasoned in mustard oil), but perhaps because of the weather, they also offer us a pile of assorted cookies. Though we are each allotted our seats, we take turns to stand by the window at the back of the room and stare out at the cloud-hung valley beyond. I can catch a glimpse of it from the window above what used to be Diana's bed. It is the only slice of a spectacular view that we are able to glimpse. I make a mental note to ask if I can shift to the now-vacant bed. In the corner, with the window opening out to the Himalayan range, it doesn't feel quite so cave-like.

By the evening session, my breath rests on the flow of air within my nose at least some of the time. I am beginning to understand why the monks or sadhus moved higher into the mountains for their tapasya. The air running into your nostril stings chill, and the air coming out, processed by the inhalation of your body, is warm. I remember doing this as a child in my bed in the southern mountains of Kodaikanal. My mother in the other room, my brother in boarding school, my father overseas, and wild boar and howling wolves foraging in the vegetable patch next door from the dense shola beyond. Too scared of the dark to make a sound, or switch on a light, I would lay there thinking about how the cold air went in, but what came out was warm, imagining it to be the Gulf stream off the coast of Newfoundland described in my school textbook. In the gap between the incoming breath and the outgoing breath lies focus. Without it, I would probably have taken much longer to still the mind. For now, I am glad I have been a child of the mountains. As my thoughts follow that stream, I am filled with a warm gratitude for my life.

The day hasn't thrown up too much angst for me, except that my limbs are not as supple as I imagined them to be. Excruciating pain shoots up and down my forelegs, protesting like communists against money. I actually expected the pins and needles, but this is outright rebellion in the ranks. I try massaging them quietly with my thumb and forefingers, but you would think I took away their liquor rations. I have no choice but to keep shifting position. It seems to me as though everyone else is very still, but I am seated at the front of the hall and I cannot really tell without turning around. Neena, to my left, doesn't budge. She doesn't stir, or open her eyes. She doesn't cough and she doesn't hunch. I call her the Little Buddha in my head. To my right, my roomie, Navya, is fast asleep and snoring as she sits up again. I stretch, cough, hunch, straighten my spine again, make a face, adjust my shawl, shift to vajrasana, sitting on my knees with my ankles tucked under me, then give up and twist again into the ardhapadmasana, retie my hair into its ponytail, massage my shins and attempt to give it another go. In between are a few stolen moments of successful, undisturbed breathing.

cold air in!

By the time the gong rings us to the close of session, I am exhausted from my thoughts.

The assistant teacher seems disapproving of those of us opting for the English discourse. We will miss out the nuances of the Hindi discourse, he informs us. It is recommended I shift. The Teacher is far more eloquent in Hindi, he explains. I consider it, but while I speak passable street Hindi, the elevated language that the Teacher uses is completely lost on me. I'd rather be clear on what I am hearing. We must make our way to the smaller audiovisual room, which is on the other side of the campus reserved for men. So we are required to wait until the men have all made it to their places before the gate is unlocked. I wonder if we would call this regressive, this segregation of the sexes. Most eastern religions indulge in it. I have lived in a segregated space in my college days, also affiliated to an ashram, and I have previously called it out in my writings as sexist and impractical as a practice. I found it unnatural and, in fact, perpetuating gender divides. Here I am, putting myself through the same process again. So why am I tolerating it now? It's true it's only for ten days, and while I am here voluntarily, I must follow the rules of the sangha, the spiritual collective, if I am to give the teaching a fair chance. So, reluctantly, I set aside my rebellion for the time being. Perhaps there are messages in that that I am yet to comprehend. If this practice has been good enough for Yuval Noah Harari, it's good enough for me, I decide. Though I do reserve a suspicion that he may get more attention than we nobodies do. I'm pretty sure he's in a cosy cell in the gold-tipped pagoda in Manori Island, off the coast of Mumbai, and has one-to-one sessions with a senior assistant teacher. As we enter the mini-hall, I am relieved that the space is a little more relaxed in that we may lean against the wall. Exhausted, we all do, even as a little whitewash rubs off on us. The sevika and the (male) sevak bow to the television again. I cannot bring myself to do so and wonder if I will ever be the kind of person who does. I find it decidedly odd – how we willingly worship just about anything.

The Day 1 discourse begins. The Teacher has a sense of humour, and that helps. He seems to know all the questions initiates like me have on the first day. He's accumulated them all and the discourse is one long funny but comprehensive answer. He even mentions the cold air coming in and the warm air going out. It feels nice to know that I am on the right track. Like getting a star on your first assignment. My energy perks right back up and I am pleased with myself. On this

7. Warm air out

course, all that is unknown to you about yourself must become known to you – the ugliness, the selfishness, the goodness, the resilience – all. Respiration becomes the bridge from the known self to the unknown. I sheepishly make a mental note to dial down the smugness. There are only two countries of residence for the mind: the past and the future. The trick is to bring it to rest in the present. If a human being behaved or spoke outwardly the way the mind does – jumping incoherently from point to point, weeping at a memory one minute and inflamed with anticipation the next – we would categorize them as insane. Taming this insanity is the work of meditation. Some of us are laughing a bit too loudly, maybe because it relieves some of the stress of having tried so hard all day.

That night, I am too tired to miss dinner as my head hits the pillow. I have drawn back the curtain between my own and the now-vacant bed to my left, so I can look out of the window. The room is fading and I can make out the silhouette of a mountain range in the distance.

The roomie is signalling with her torch in the dark. She's either wishing me goodnight or it's code for help. I'm too far gone to respond to either.

Day 2

Fizzy Like Cola

DAWN IS FILTERING IN THROUGH THE CRACKS between the exhaust fan blades in the main meditation hall when the whistling thrush begins to sing. He is calm and pointed, as if singing to a specific lover across the valley. Clarity uplifts his voice with a distinct note, above the accumulated vocabulary of his trilling brethren. I listen to him until the light changes from dull grey to a delicate gold. For the next ten days, the gaps between the exhaust fan and the rhythms of the birds tell me the time of day. We sit facing the front of the hall, which, save for the interruption of the fan, is one stark facade of plywood upon cement, painted white and blue. One set of windows to the right is hung with blackout curtains that will never be parted. We are not here for the view, I realize. How strange when all the marketeers of meditation sell you svelte yoga practitioners on the edge of mountain streams and on pristine hilltops. It's such a long con. To a serious practitioner, the view is only one more distraction. You could be by the sea, atop the Himalayas or in a forest – it shouldn't matter. You meditate with your eyes shut anyway. The only view you must be offered is the one within. If you must go somewhere, go for the silence. It occurs to me that for every Indian guru who may have offered a genuinely revelatory practice to the West, savvy brand builders have sold meditation in vacation retreats in one long scam. I am not trying too hard this morning. I simply surrender to the sounds around me and the thoughts bubbling up within me. The upper lip, where my attention is focused, seems to be set at a gentle simmer.

You don't notice that the nape of your nostril is burning until they ask you to feel for it. When they do, perhaps it is the gentle power of suggestion, but there it is. A gentle throb and a glow. Everyone feels it differently. For some it tingles, for others it tickles, and some don't feel anything at all. Mine feels as though I applied too much Vicks menthol rub out of a jar. The assistant teacher, taking notes, is asking us to describe what we are feeling in threes. He looks startled at my description and bursts into a small laugh. I am flustered. I am so convinced that this is what I feel. 'Is that not a valid sensation? Am I doing it wrong?' I ask. 'All sensations are valid sensations as long as they are sensations,' he replies. I get that. To feel at all in a world like this, let alone feel minutely, is an accomplishment. It is probably a truer feeling than all the things we claim to feel – anger, love, passion, duty, fear, outrage – throughout our social media preoccupation. I observe the burning to see if it will change. Perhaps a tickle would be nice. An itch? Someone said it feels like crawling insects or ants. Oh god, I hope I don't feel that! Oops! No gods here. Hehe.

I avoid looking at Navya through breakfast, though I can sense she is trying to catch my eye. I am avoiding her so studiously she now pointedly wants to catch my eye to ask me if I am okay. We are locked in a cycle of avoidance now. We have all surreptitiously checked out Diana and her foot, which seems to be swollen from a prior injury in Thailand. She is unable to sit cross-legged on it and has been requesting a chair. I think about Jessica, frail and clearly unable to cope with the pain. I see her clutch her knees between her arms when I get up to use the bathroom mid-session, but she buries her curly-topped head between them and asks for nothing, or rather, doesn't get it. When both of them come from the same circumstance and face the same cultural differences, why is one of them in a single room and seeking a chair and the other not? I contemplate karma and past life deeds, and how it creates different levels of impact and tolerance, forming associations out of thin air. I take my time sauntering back from the toilet, open the screen door of our room to put some cream on my crackly nose – must be all the heat, I chuckle to myself – and crane my neck to seek the top of the mountain we are on before I step back into the hall.

It is a gorgeously sunny day, but that does not justify the amount of heat my body is generating. I peel off my shawl and roll it up. It stuffs neatly between my foot and shin, so it eases the pain a little. It's insufficient though. I take off my jacket in half an hour. I can feel the sweat starting to run down my thighs. I am deeply disturbed by this. My first thought is that I am having a hot flash. While my doctor asked me to prepare for menopause, it is still too soon. Surely, I have another three or four years to go. I discreetly touch my forehead to check if I have a fever that I have not noticed. My bronchitis has been acting up due to the altitude but nothing a few puffs of the inhaler hasn't been able to handle. I don't particularly feel feverish though. I look around. Everyone is bundled up in layers. It is only me feeling this incredible wave of heat. When I am able to focus, the meditation goes well. My breath is smooth and clear. The burning sensation is distinct. I feel I am starting to get the hang of this.

I have a new game to play with myself. I notice the stock of vegetables placed on a counter in a shed outside the kitchen door. Piles of pumpkins, beans, brinjals and gourds, radishes, leafy greens and ladies' fingers. It is the ration for the entire course. Every day a different pile diminishes a little. Every day I guess what's for lunch and what will be for the next day's meals. Except for the potatoes, onions and pulses, the options in the store are visible. I award myself points for guessing correctly. Sure enough, it is the pointy brinjal today, broad beans and more chickpeas.

I am amazed that some of the women wash their hair every other day even in this weather. We have taken to setting chairs out in the gap between the porch and the stone wall and sitting, not facing each other, not

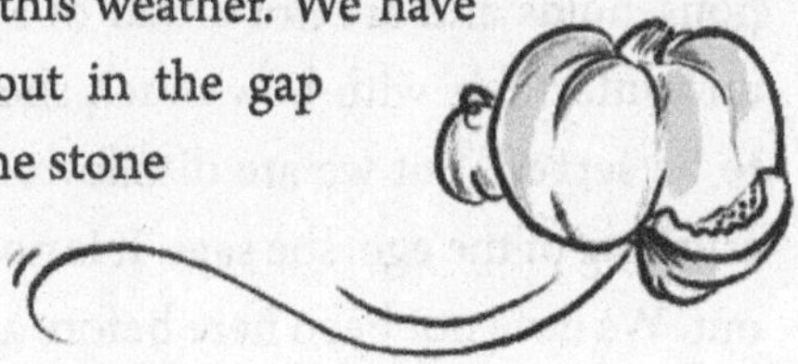

speaking, not even looking at one another, but together. It is a strange, silent bond that only women are capable of forming. Some dry their hair, others their washed clothes, undergarments, air out their blankets and sweaters, others stretch their legs out to ease the pain in their limbs. Some pace, tired of sitting. Srijana does lunges against the steps, though that is not permitted; but we do not stop her. We know how it is. Neena is here too, staring at her feet. When Ana stands up and unravels her top knot, she reveals waist-length hair that can filter the sun. Navya shivers even in the afternoon and retires to bed. Jessica embraces herself, protecting herself from something so harsh we each wish we could will it away. Dechen sweeps the house front and cleans the toilets. She does not allow us to help her. Raima attempts to take the broom and sweep alongside, but is reprimanded. Dechen lugs jerrycans of hot water to refill our dispenser, so we are kept supplied at all times. She pins the agenda and sutta, for the day to the noticeboard. And then she serves us our meals and may only eat after we have finished. It seems unnecessarily arduous and we are more than willing to pull our weight. Most of us are older women who run full-fledged households and are not afraid of a little hard work. We are uncomfortable with how much she does. We do not expect to be served. But we are disallowed. This is her service, her crushing of the ego, she says. It is not permitted for us to help out. We have not been here before and she has, several times, so we believe her and must step back. At most, we may sweep beneath and around our beds, so we do what we can, washing out the bathrooms after we use them, so that there will be less to do for Dechen, whom we are each becoming concentric to, orbs in our own worlds, overlapping each other's.

Though I have contributed no physical labour to the chores of the day, here I am, sweating in the 7°C afternoon for no reason whatsoever.

The session immediately after lunch should give us the freedom to meditate in our rooms. But my roomie snores, so I'm sitting outside and gazing at the mountain as others sleep surreptitiously. Finding us in states that range from daydreaming to sleeping, i.e. distinctly not meditation, the assistant teacher, exercising his discretion, orders us all back to the hall without exception. My afternoon session today is not going very well.

I feel like a shaken bottle of cola, with the fizzy bubbles erupting through me, each carrying effervescent memories of people and events that have scarred my life. Men I shouldn't have loved, women I shouldn't have trusted, places I should never have gone, jobs I shouldn't have quit, words I shouldn't have said, words that shouldn't have been said to me that I shouldn't be latching on to all these years later. It flows – a litany of betrayal. I think of them up and down and backwards and forwards, and chronologically and in order of severity, steeped in an intense sense of having been wronged. Parents, siblings, children, exes, friends and their accoutrements of lovers, exes and the never-ending extension of antagonists parade themselves on a spotlit stage. That gossipy aunt and this blackmailing editor. That prying landlord and this tormenting in-law. The abusive ex, the thieving boyfriend, the impotent lover, the best friend who wasn't. Every time the bubbles get more furious, I open my eyes to release myself from thinking about the people they bring into view. I rearrange myself and begin again. Twenty minutes later, there I am again, meandering through a Sophoclean chorus of wrongs and rights, joys and pains, people I miss and people I had forgotten about. I am consumed by my own left turns. I turn over the possibilities of my own alternate history. How different my life would have been had I made other choices, and taken the opportunities I didn't, and declined those I did. Should have married the NRI classmate of my brother who came home with a proposal when I was already dating the man I would later marry. Or that banker dude from Hong Kong. But then, my son wouldn't have been born, would he? I keep trying to bring my mind back to my breath, but too much has been stirred up. I have spent a lifetime trying to keep this pain down, to release, to forget. It has been exhausting. It occurs to me that these condensed emotions form the bricks of rammed earth that build the walls between ourselves. The only real way to release ... is to feel. I am at peak fizz and the only way to be emptied of these bubbles is to stop shaking the bottle. I give up trying. Give up trying not to feel, to feel, to respond in any way. I let go and watch the churn bring the scum to the surface.

It is around three in the afternoon, the sun through the fan blades seems west of centre, when something begins to shift. I have been thinking of my son, his journey from cherubic childhood to angst-ridden teenager. From secretly popping notes in my handbag to tell me he loved me, to shouting that he hates me when asked to pick up his towel. I have responded with as much hurt and anger, using control where I should have simply used love. The more the people you love hurt you, the more you build walls to separate yourself from yourself. The fizz stills and the walls within begin to collapse. I feel it as keenly as a house crumbling around me in an earthquake. I sit there, watching everything around me begin to dissolve. Except, this is inside. My stomach feels a churn and a shift, a physical sensation as though I am going to vomit. A band in my forehead, the accumulated and unexpressed stress of decades, tightens till it feels physical. In one swift movement, it snaps and the sensation moves from the pit of my stomach violently upwards. It happens within a matter of seconds, and as I watch, horrified, a huge sob bursts involuntarily out of my mouth. As it gurgles out, it glues together all the tyrannies I believe have been inflicted upon me, and what emerges is the one isolated truth – that none of it really matters. That everything I have endured, every choice I have made, right or wrong, I did to protect and provide for my son as a single mother. And I would do it all over again. Nothing has ever been more important, and no one has been as relevant. Truth be told, I have never loved any man because none measured up to the love of my life – my child. I have been guilty of self-sabotaging those whom I might have ended up in a commitment with, because I marked them down as less of a priority. I am as guilty of toying with them, these strings of broken relationships that were never meant to go anywhere, as they have been with me. Because they didn't matter to me. They never have. An inability to understand this about myself has made me put myself in positions I didn't want to be in for the wrong reasons – perceived stability, social pressure and self-imposed beliefs about where I ought to be at that time in my life. I subsequently exited them in a hasty and ill-conceived manner, making poor choices that ended up affecting what actually mattered to me – the ability to earn and provide for the person I did care about. So many ideas I have harboured about myself, about those I feel wronged by, and those whom I have wronged, become apparent in that moment. The intricate chain of cause and effect by which I have taken specific actions and reaped logical consequences, even while I wished for other outcomes, is made evident to me.

As the consummate weeping begins to unleash itself, it centres on the end of this era of motherhood. In a few months, my son will turn eighteen and leave for college. I have lived and endured for him for so long that without him I will have to rediscover an identity separate from all this blame and duty. The teenager who now stands on the threshold of a life I hope I have prepared him for, whose love is unconditional, but who at the same time sees my flaws deeply – does he leave knowing how much I love him? More than the cumulative horror of anything that I have had to face in the world? What sense of me, or what sense of home, does he leave with? Or have I damaged him in some way, triggering in him the same need to escape that I had as a teenager, and have only just understood? I do not want him to spend his life acting with the same motivations I had, and not understanding them.

I rush out of the hall in a panic as the flood of tears bursts forth. I am now shaking violently. This is no gentle crying of the distressed. This is an earth-shaking weeping of the devastated. I have not witnessed something like this in myself before. I rush up the thirty-odd stairs to my room and pull my towel out of my suitcase. My face is red and the sobs have now turned into open bawling. I cry like my heart is broken. I can feel a dam of tears held back for most of my adult life gush through the crack in the wall until there is no edifice left standing. I sob for myself, for my son, for those who have hurt me and those I have hurt. I sob for time lost and opportunities sold. I sob for outcomes I cannot control, for enmities harboured and friendships broken. I sob for those who understood me and those who didn't. I sob for love. I sob for hate. I sob until I am empty. The neat compartments of the separate selves are dissolved. I do not know where I am or how long I have been here. My eyes are swelling up and I can barely open them. When I regain a sense of my surroundings, a worried Dechen is standing near my bed. I have been sobbing so copiously that a sizeable number of our small contingent of women has made excuses of using the washroom or drinking water and rushed to my door, and is pacing outside worriedly, unable to ask if I am okay. Diana has anxiously come with a glass of water and she attempts to pat my head. I shrink back, not wanting to be touched. She apologizes and rushes out. 'It is good, it is normal,' Dechen promises me. 'I too have cried several times. It is what needs release. Don't hold back. Come back to the hall,' she says. I look at her stunned. 'I don't want to disturb the whole room and I am not able to stop crying,' I say. I am a little annoyed, truth be told. Can't they let me have my privacy at this moment? She insists. 'The vibrations are stronger in the hall and that which needs to be exorcized will be released faster.' She leaves me to collect myself. My hand towel is soaking wet by now. Reassured, my sangha takes itself back to the hall.

I am alone now. I wait for the last footsteps to recede. I go to the washroom and run cold water over my face. I drink some water. I lie down for a few minutes. I feel wrung out, it is true, but I also feel miraculously light, lighter than I can last remember. Perhaps I was like this as a child, when I felt unfettered excitement for an outing, when I didn't know bad things could happen. I have been running for eighteen years, too afraid to stop, too afraid to break down in case I never start up again. I let the still fall on me and steep in it before I make my way to the hall again. The tears are still streaming, but these are gentler – a process of physical elimination that tells me it will continue in the background, like a heartbeat, until its work is done. This time I carry my towel with me.

As I take my seat, the assistant teacher calls me to sit in front of him. This is my first one-to-one, an exception mid-session. My body is still heaving from the impact of the violent outburst. Calm is some breaths away.

'What is the problem?' he asks.

'Nothing,' I say.

'Nothing?'

'Nothing.'

I am not able to pinpoint any one reason why I am crying. At least, there is nothing that he can solve for me.

'Then why are you crying?' he asks.

'I am crying because I cannot stop crying,' I say.

He laughs. 'People cry for all kinds of little reasons, and here you are crying without a reason.'

'Is that not valid?' I ask.

'That is valid. You are crying tears even you cannot see and that you did not know you were carrying the burden of. This usually happens later for some people – it has happened earlier for you. That is good. Let it all out,' he says. 'Cry as much as you need to.'

all sensations are valid

I return to my seat wishing I had one of those solvable problems – the longing for a better room, a softer pillow, a nicer job, a larger home, a cure for this terrible leg ache. These are the fixable ones. A balm here, a better job there, a relocation there. They are problems with identifiable solutions. I have problems I don't even know I have. How on earth will I fix them? At least, I think as I go back to my breath, I now know that no fear or confrontation is or has been more important to me than the welfare of my son. So knowing what is not important, let's start from there. It is easy to release then the things that we hold on to but don't need to. I know I want my son to not hate me for my flaws. I want him to not judge me. I want him to know I love him. That I will always support him. The rest are nebulous details. I also have mysteriously lost the sense of blame I feel towards all my perceived antagonists. It all feels fated and purposeful, these missteps, theirs and mine equally, to the end. What is important to me is intact. Little else matters.

With this realization comes an incredible heat that radiates from my body from the inward out. I feel the glow bursting through the pores of my cheeks, my forehead, my ears. It has been a whole day and I have not been able to wear warm clothing. I know now this is no hot flash. It is a cellular release. Physically and mentally, I feel scrubbed over. Free.

The sutta for Day 2 has been the Ratana Sutta, a paritta (protective) verse said to be chanted by the Buddha during a famine in the city of Vaishali. It is drawn from the Sutta Nipāta (verse 2.1), one of the oldest and most popular texts of the miscellaneous collection of the Khuddhaka-nikāya.

> Sahāvassa dassana-sampadāya,
> tayassu dhammā jahitā bhavanti;
> sakkāyadiṭṭhi vicikicchithaṃ ca,
> silabbataṃ vāpi yadatthi kiñci.
>
> With the attainment of the first Path,
> three things are abandoned in him:

illusion of self, doubt,
and [clinging to] rites and rituals and such things.

Religions promise us salvation as though it were an object to be gifted to you, like Santa checking the naughty or nice list. According to the whim of those in charge. In fact, the Teacher says, your liberation is in your own hands. I think about Nirmala, a middle-aged woman whom I had employed as a caregiver to my son, then barely three, while I was at work. Every now and then, she would take ten days off to attend a vipassana course. This was already over a decade ago and I wonder how much she would have advanced by now. Maybe she is even an assistant teacher. Despite my apparent privilege – she was a widow with a teenaged daughter to bring up, and I was freshly divorced and a single mother to my son, and while we were both struggling to keep it together, I had the higher income – I did not feel so privileged at the time. I recollect that I was still nursing a sense of injustice done to me and she was already so highly evolved in her spiritual practice. The universality of dhamma and its accessibility to anyone who is willing to do the work stands in huge contrast to practices that ask the student to be worthy. I look at my roomie, who has gone back to sleep next to me and wonder if that is wise. What if someone was merely here to follow a fad? Out of curiosity? And didn't follow the rules? Wouldn't that be such a waste of both the teacher's and the student's time, or worse, a disservice to the more earnest students? There are, after all, global celebrities now taking to it with abandon. Fadsters will follow suit. Should there not be some entry norms to ensure that only those who actually want to learn, who are willing to subject themselves to this excruciating process, come here to learn? Not I, of course – I've wanted to do it ever since my nanny and, shortly after, my brother did the course. My ego is careful to nail down that important distinction in superiority as I ponder if some should be worthy of initiation.

Day 2 is the day of the silas. Morality. As initiates into dhamma, we are required to take vows not to kill, not to steal, not to consume intoxicants, and to refrain from sexual misconduct and lies. For senior students of vipassana, it will include not eating at the wrong time, not using luxurious beds and refraining from ornamentation. We will, of course, variously break these vows once we leave the premises, but while we are here, we must uphold these precepts for the teaching to work. It is the basis of dhamma. Dechen says, to her, dhamma is simply compassion, being a better human being. It's kind of untranslatable as a concept. Dhamma seems to me at once sanctuary and principle. The morality extends not just to our own conduct but also to that which we instil in others by our actions. If we sell guns, or encourage the killing of animals or men, though we may not take these actions ourselves, we are still culpable. I find these prospects daunting. I do eat chicken and fish, and by doing so I am compelling other men to earn a livelihood by killing these animals. In the larger cycle of life, I am culpable. In many small ways, throughout our day, we are each culpable. The remedy for the organic lack of sila is the repeated practice of samadhi, concentration. Not just any concentration, but concentration in the right way. This is why the Jains have a sense of contrition for the deaths they cause in the everyday aspects of living. If one cannot live without causing harm, one can at least live with the knowledge that one is causing harm. We've heard this so many times – from scriptures, wise men, parents and just good old common sense on how to live our best lives. Do right, don't cause harm. But few tell us how. We just try. And more often than not, we rely on a resolve that fails us when we need it the most. Awareness is more potent than action sometimes. Perhaps, more than the knowledge of perfection, the knowledge of our imperfection, of where and how we fail, is impactful.

I have shifted to the bed closer to the window today. There is inherent surprise in my roomie parting the curtain to realize that I am no longer next to her. She flashes her torch at the ceiling twice now. The gesture is a combination of several words: saying goodnight and asking if I am okay, if I am ready for bed and can she, being nearest the light switch, turn off the light. I tap twice on the wood of the wall next to me. I am curter and less verbose than she is. But that's all she needs. Lights out.

Day 3

The Birth of Compassion

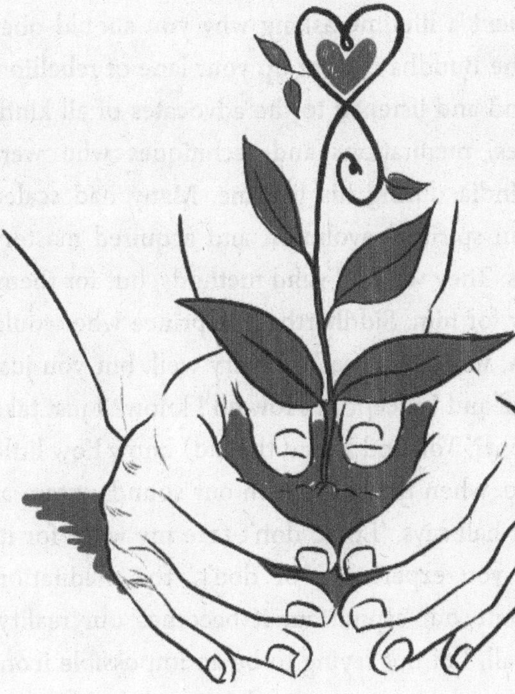

I HAVE BROUGHT UP A PRECOCIOUS KID TO THE soundtrack of 'But why?' I have bitten back many 'Because I said so!'s and have had to remind myself that it was I who taught him never to accept an instruction without questioning it. They turn on you if you teach them to think for themselves, they do. You have been warned. If you have spent a lifetime asking why you should obey people, then the Buddha is right up your lane of rebellion. He went around and listened to the advocates of all kinds of philosophies, meditations and techniques who were preaching in India during his lifetime. Many had scaled great heights in spiritual evolution and acquired mastery over the senses. They were all valid methods, but for them, not necessarily for him. Siddhartha, the prince who would be the Buddha, was like, 'That's all very well, but you just tell me this stuff and I accept it? How do I know? I just take you at your word?' You and I (and the kid) know how little that washes. So, when the teacher on our sound system at the meditation hall says, 'Look, don't take my word for it, go with what you experience, or don't,' the meditation does not become our aspiration; it becomes our reality. Here, in this hall, I'm not trying to be an impossible icon, a man or woman in the image of god, because, let's face it, who could? None of us who know our deepest flaws believe we're actually getting there. When we grasp the distance so seemingly insurmountable between ourselves and this perfect being, whichever one we may choose to believe in, we don't really bother trying. 'Enlightenment,' Thich Nhat Hanh said, 'is when the wave realizes it is the ocean.' We spend our lifetimes aspiring to be something other than who or what we are – we admire the ocean, and seek someday to be as vast, as deep, as expansive. When there is nothing to be, inasmuch as we exist, we already are. Here, somehow the most comforting message is that it's enough to be me, just so long as I take some time to know the real me.

I spend the pre-dawn hour challenging my mind. If the menthol-rub sensation on my nose is for real, it should be there even when my mind wanders and returns to the spot of focus. I take my thoughts on walkabouts to test out my theory. Not that I need an excuse. Each time I return, the sensation is still there.

My body and I get into a smooth rhythm even as we spar in this way. It has been three days of sitting in ardhapadmasana for fifteen hours a day. We have come to know each other intimately in a way that only strangers delicately intertwined limb to limb in a jammed suburban train compartment in peak hour will know. We know the reek of each other's armpits at the end of a long day, as it were. There are no niceties left between us. I recognize my body's fatigue and its crankiness. It has its mood swings, much like I do, and we are beginning to recognize each other through the filter of our moods. It says it is fine when I know it is not. I quietly massage it to painlessness, but then put it through a torturous routine of contortion. We tell each other we're going to get through this difficult hour, but we both know we are not. We are going to hit that same old speed bump three quarters into the morning meditation and it's going to be the same fight all over again. It is going to sulk. I am going to try to tug it back into a good mood. I will fail and storm out, shifting to another position while it nurses itself to feel better. Then we reset and restart. We are in a stormy, mutually dissatisfying relationship.

As with any such, our options are to end it, live with the pain or come to an agreement. Like a warring couple who only realize the ways in which they have grown apart during therapy, it has taken me three days to realize my body and I are far from aligned. At some rare moments during the sessions, we find ourselves in sync, and we are able to achieve rare progress. If I thought of us as one of those grey-haired couples in step on their morning walks, I have looked closer and realized one of us is hard of hearing and the other sullen in communication. We are learning to speak to each other again.

We have no choice but to come to an agreement. The secret only the therapist knows is that what one partner views as a happy compromise, the other views as an imposition. I hold out hope that at some point during this course, my body will provide me a painless meditation. My body sniggers with a prescience I lack. I am going to have to compromise too. Harmony is not just me getting my way. Compromise means the body is going to get its way too. Pain therefore is going to be inevitable.

In time, I will learn that I am in no position to snap at it to stop generating or feeling or expressing its pain. The only thing I have probably done for decades is to not hear its pain. Now, here, I owe it a fair listening. I have thought to myself if I was on a chair I would not hurt. I contemplate asking if I can stand at the back of the hall and meditate. But this is not the kind of agony that simply goes away when you change your position. If it was so, Diana or Aunty Pradhan, who have been assigned chairs, would be free of pain. You could lie down, or stretch out, and you would still not be free of this pain. Nobody in this process is ever free of the pain. The pain is an inextricable part of our mutual self-discovery. It has begun to redefine our relationship.

I am still recovering from my outburst of the day before. Truth be told, I am sheepish at my public meltdown. I feel naked and exposed. If my sangha thought me a sensible woman before the course began, do they think me pretentious, weak and undignified now? Perhaps they pity me, and think I have suffered deeply in life. I am used to being thought of as a strong woman. I wear the facade like an armour. I am, more than I care to admit, preoccupied by how I must have seemed to them – this howling banshee of a woman, windswept by emotions I didn't know I had. Keeping it together is a prime lesson of not just womanhood, and motherhood, but of adulthood, employment and productivity. Every time that I have allowed myself my weaknesses, I have been punished for it. Some of what I feel today is also fear. What will follow the vulnerability? The lessons that came with it are still accumulating to a point of revelation.

Just because I have arrived at a recognition of the irrelevance of any particular person or set of persons in the larger pattern of my life, does what transpired between us cease to impact me? I am revisited by long-buried memories of multiple hospital visits, a difficult pregnancy at the age of twenty-four, being abandoned in a strange city. I remember the feeling of being hit. The distorted face of he who stood over me shouting, 'I'll go to jail if I have to, but I will kill you first!' Of suicide attempts. Of returning to a space of hurt because I was left with no other options. Of escape. Of stalking. Blank calls. Bullying. Sneering. Character assassination. Of anger, betrayal, disappointment, fear. I still feel the fear. Each emotion, whether derived from a buried impulse or a fresh one, continues to overwhelm me.

In daily life, I deal with these deep hurts by refusing to allow myself to dwell on them, because they disturb me,

and the past has no solution. I wrap them in old newspaper and put them in a box marked 'Do Not Open' on a shelf in the attic. This is how I get on with the rest of my life. Here, we are in the middle of Diwali cleaning, and the cleanse is thorough. Nothing remains unopened. That which you bury leaves its bare bones behind. That which you burn reincarnates, taking on another life of its own. Everything is energy, positive and negative, and energy never goes away. It remains or returns in another form. I release any illusion of control. I can only watch my thoughts bubble up, and dissolve, each into another emotion, another feeling, another memory. I may wince a little, but I am veering towards a 'you don't scare me' bravado. I watch them come and go, come and go, like waves, melting into each other as soon as they hit the shore. Anger, sorrow, despair, fear, rage, joy, tenderness, wistfulness, lost longing – dissolving, each no different from the other. While on Day 1 the monkey mind was my burden, today it has reincarnated into a blessing. Because thankfully nothing, not even pain, stays forever.

It seems like a small revelation, but it comes as a huge relief. As I witness each emotion as a reaction to what X said and Y did, I also see clearly that I took actions as a result of those emotions. I am summed up like a perfectly balanced mathematical equation. Every action in them created a reaction in me. Every reaction in me created an action in me. Every action in me created a reaction in another. We are each, they and I and they, linked in a daisy chain formed by children playing ignorantly, not quite innocently, in a meadow on a summer's day.

When confronted with hostile situations or people, I have felt threatened – I reacted with fear or anger, and I ran. I moved a house, or quit a job, I exited a friends' circle, or a professional network. I disengaged, or engaged myself elsewhere. I chose partners not as absolute choices in themselves, but to prevent myself from returning to what I was leaving behind. I picked options that reaffirmed my disappointments. A man who would, by default, bear the blame for the relationship not working out. A job that I never saw myself gain expertise in ten years down the line. How could it succeed when I never wanted it to? That was not its purpose. Its purpose was to put the past in its place. I have jumped from life raft to life raft, never building or finding myself a ship going to where I wanted to go. You don't even pause to think of where you want to go when you are merely surviving. I have blamed the ocean for the turbulence. To self-sabotage is an instinct that preserves you from dealing with an outcome you didn't want to begin with. I was there to escape those who went before, maybe even punish them, and validate my judgements about how unreliable they each were, as though doing that in some way freed me from taking the blame.

Whenever I have travelled down paths I chose for the wrong reasons, I have invariably had to stop and correct my course. I blamed fate or the actions of others for the resulting instability. I used anger and self-righteousness to manipulate outcomes. I evicted the non-compliant. I found obstacles to reject opportunities. All the while playing the victim, and believing myself to be so. Each of those reactions pushed me further away from healing my wounds. Instead, they perpetuated a new line of action that invited newer inflictions. Thus was embroidered a pattern of disappointment and its affirmation.

I see now that nobody failed me. Nobody can fail us. We choose our outcomes through our reactions. Economists believe we are never without choice. Well, the Buddha says we are never compelled to choose.

Here I am, twenty years later, continuing down this trajectory of action and reaction.

We still must act every day. When you take an action as an absolute in itself, its motivation and genesis is self-contained. Thus, it becomes self-fulfilling. I see now that any action taken merely as a reaction to a past action cannot have a positive result. It cannot, in fact, have a result different from what it was taken for. What is it that they say about nothing really going away until it has taught you what it has to? Actually, nothing goes away until you stop reacting to it.

If the meditation is working, then it will confer an immediate clarity. I understand now what Moses means when he describes how the sea parted. It is a lifting of the fog. We have been sold the idea that this mythical clarity will come with a strong beam of light streaming down from the sky, with the music of harps and violins serenading our path, along which we will now float through life. These are metaphors. The Buddha keeps it quite simple. What you see is your action and your reaction, where it came from and where it led to. Thus, the path, where you came from and where you will go, is clear. When you finally see it, that is quite sufficient.

The Enlightened see the origin of this chain long before birth, stretching into previous lifetimes, and long after, stretching into the future. They see what has to stop to end the infinite cycle. Quite simply, this is liberation.

I am not there. I will not be for a long time, probably many lifetimes. I see that too. For me, here and now, it suffices to know, in a string of brief and specific events, how to stop dragging this burden along. If our minds are monkeys, we spend our lives dancing to the tune of the music box every time someone turns the key. The solution is simple: stop dancing. That one can simply choose to do so is an astonishing revelation. It shouldn't be. The only person I have to blame for every hostile reaction or not-so-satisfactory outcome is me.

This is immensely useful to me in measures of simple life choices. I have been contemplating relocating out of Mumbai for quite a few years. I simply haven't been able to pinpoint where I will move to. Sometimes I think I will move to Delhi, because it will be 'good for my career'. At other times I think Dubai, to make some money and kick those savings up a notch. Sometimes I want a house in the mountains, and have asked an elderly couple I often live with in McLeod Ganj to let me know if anything in the vicinity comes up for sale. I have, at various points, asked the boss to let me know if there are vacancies in bureaus in Mysore, Pune, Madurai and Goa (that last one is on everyone's list, I bet). Liechtenstein is also a nice option. I watch relocation reality shows and my list expands. Each a castle on a cloud more ephemeral than the other. As the chain of cause and effect jumps into view like one of those viral domino videos of bricks in a wall, the pieces of my life fall into place. All I have known is that I must move. I have not known why the urge to move is so strong. The truth sticks out at me like a leg stuck out to trip me up from a smirking fellow sitting on a rock by the side of a path I ran down because I thought I had lost him a long way behind. I am still running from him and I don't even know it.

If I continue running without knowing why, I will always have to rectify the outcome. I still want to move, but now I know the wrong reasons to take that step. The right reasons are in future meditations, and will emerge with self-contained outcomes for myself. This meditation now is about neither the past nor the future, but the present. When you have disentangled yourself from the circuitous road of the past, you are free to arrive, unfettered, at your now.

My present for now is simply a leg screaming bloody murder. While I have been travelling down a chain of my thoughts, my lower limbs have come to the brink of disengaging themselves from my torso.

The good thing with being in a high-altitude centre is that there is no such thing as too many pee breaks. I take them, we all do, to stretch our legs. I use a drink of water as an excuse – as a result, I am more hydrated than I have ever been. When I reach the rooms, Raima, unable to stand Dechen not allowing her to help, is secretly, and with a stubborn and defensive set of her jaw, sweeping the steps and porch. I look away so as not to make her feel self-conscious. I stand with a glass of hot water in my hand in one of the walkways and look out at the accumulated clouds over the obscured mountaintops. On clear days, you can see Gangtok and the brightly coloured roofs of small-scale industrial units in the valley below. The hot water seems to drive its own paths to clarity as if it were melting accumulated snow. I make a mental note to drink more of it when I get home. I wonder how long I am going to stick with the many resolutions I am making here.

Back in the hall, roomie Navya, who used to sit next to me, has moved a row behind because the light above her head disturbs her. The kindly assistant teacher assumes that means her meditations. I suspect it is more her sleep. I instantly feel embarrassed at this uncharitable judgement I am making. I want to make excuses for myself. It is coming from too much proximity. I am used to having my own space. I feel so intruded upon, so I am reacting with irritation to the object of the unsuspecting intrusion. This has little to do with her. She is a doctor and probably rarely sleeps well when on duty. She is here, she is trying, she is present, which is more than one can say for many. I return to my seat, understanding how deeply flawed a human being I am. It is difficult to realize this, those of us who like to think of ourselves as essentially good people. This meditation is no ego-massage trip.

How have I been so stupid all my life? This is the question I want to lead with when I seek audience with the assistant teacher at the noontime question hour. I suspect he may not have an answer for me though. I'll have to figure that one out myself. Instead, I ask about my breath. My bronchitis is starting to kick in due to the altitude. Consequently, every breath is short and inadequate. Every fourth breath requires me to inhale deeply, to fill my lungs. When I do focus on my breath, it thus becomes an intentional breath, not a regular one. What is regular for me periodically is the deep breath to fill my lungs. 'Stop wondering if others' normal ought to be your normal,' the assistant teacher replies. 'Your normal is what is normal for you alone.' I understand that in meditation, as in hospitals, we count in units of one.

Today the Little Buddha is wearing a beautiful batik floral black-and-white flared palazzo that forms a half circle around her when she grabs the edges and stretches them out with her arms. Standing there in the sun, her eyes closed, her neck elongated such that her face is tilted up to the sky, she is a bird of paradise in full bloom, so radically altered from her diminutive persona.

By the afternoon session, I understand compassion a bit better. To begin with, it starts with oneself. Compassion for my own mistakes, all those wrong turns and why I took them. Compassion is not making excuses for my flaws; it is acknowledging and seeing them, in their entirety – why I made them, what my motivations were, what would push me to repeat them, what I have to give myself to stop making them. If I have compassion for myself upon realizing that my string of actions is but reactions, well, it follows, so are the actions of others. If I reacted to things my mother said to me as a teenager, my mother was reacting to things her husband or in-laws said or did to her. As the cycle procreates, it also finds its progenitors, infinitely at both ends. We are all each trapped in this propagation of action and reaction, each its victim, each its perpetrator. The actions I have taken as reactions will propel another, maybe my son, to react similarly, just as I have, spawning his own cycle of cause and effect.

The thought fills me with horror. I want to get out of here in this instant and call him. I want to apologize for disproportionate anger, for decisions taken for him that had nothing to do with what was best for him, and for not always being able to predict or control an outcome. At the same time, I see that those who acted with violence against me were not in control of their own outcomes, could not have predicted my reactions, controlled or even countered them, and thus have suffered equally.

The sutta for Day 3 is the Karaṇífiyametta Sutta or the Metta Sutta, the sutta of compassion, with an additional verse added to it in the paritta tradition that uses verses protectively, to ward off misfortune or danger. It occurs in both the Khuddakapātha, the first collection of discourses in the Khuddhaka-nikāya, and the Sutta Nipāta (verse 1.8). It advocates love towards all beings.

Mātā yathā niyam puttaṃ,
āyusā ekaputtamanurakkhe;

evampi sabbabhūtesu
mānasaṃ bhāvaye aparimāṇaṃ

Just as a mother would protect her only child
with her own life,
even so let us cultivate
boundless love towards all things.

Mettañca sabbalokasmim, mānasaṃ bhāvaye aparimāṇaṃ

Let one's thoughts of boundless metta (unconditional love) pervade the whole world.

Wisdom, or panna, the Teacher explains, develops in three stages. The first, sutta maya panna, received wisdom, arrives by reading or listening to the words of others. The second, cinta maya panna, intellectual wisdom, arrives by considering the received wisdom from others. The third wisdom, and the highest one, bhavana maya panna, is experiential knowledge – that which you know because you discovered, felt and experienced it. The first two are only valuable if they lead you to the third, the true wisdom.

You have to like a teacher who tells you to trust yourself above all others. I take the bowing to the TV under advisement. For today, I wholeheartedly chant along with the others when they recite 'Sadhu Sadhu Sadhu' at the end of the sessions. It means you second and acknowledge the words of the wise one you have just heard from. Like the honourable representatives of the House of the Lords thumping at their desks, we, the sangha, resound with approval for what the Teacher is saying. Every sentence you produce must be a universally applicable truth, or it is of little use to the world, he notes. I contemplate some of my favourite nuggets of Zen poetry and understand with clarity for the first time what the poet seers were saying. Taigu Ryokan sang:

> Too lazy to be ambitious
> I let the world take care of itself.
> Ten days' worth of rice in my bag;
> a bundle of twigs by the fireplace.
> Why chatter about delusion and enlightenment?
> Listening to the night rain on my roof,
> I sit comfortably, with both legs stretched out.
>
> (*Dewdrops on a Lotus Leaf*, tr. John Stevens)

I understand the sentiment. I even see what a haiku is now. Poor imitation poets have focused on the syllable structures for years when it is about the structure of the thought. You cannot arrive at simplicity so sublime unless you have released each thought from the trappings of the cyclic action and reaction chain. Only then do words become whole and sentences complete in themselves. I think of the writings of Yuval Noah Harari, and make a mental note to go back and reread all his statements to see how he executes this in page after page of very fat books. This is why his words ring so unshakeably true.

Gautama, the Buddha's experience of meditation was the technique of vipassana, an instrument that revealed to him that the true essence of the body was mutability, because at its base, it is made of kalapas. Think of them as the minutest subatomic particles. Billions of them form the bottom note of our physical structures, so subtle we cannot see them or feel them. But they exist. How do we know they do? Not just because someone tells us so. We can know this, the Teacher points out, by observing our bodies. We don't grow from infancy to adulthood overnight. We change in stages. Each of those stages is registered on the body. The growing of the fingernails, hair, the elasticity and sagging of the skin, the greying, a natural defoliation – it all goes on, whether we witness it or not. When our bodies sleep, our unconscious mind remains in control of our body. When a mosquito bites you, your hand will still rise to soothe the spot in your sleep. So if we don't consciously witness it, does it mean it doesn't happen? Or that we are inadequate witnesses? Logic would dictate the fault is at our end.

To meditate is then merely the act of sharpening the mind so that we are able to bear witness. There are many ways of meditating, and it depends on your pursuit of them which you adopt. Vipassana is accessible to all who are willing to put in the work in order to bear witness – not to miraculous outcomes, but to a clear view of the changing nature of your own mind and body.

I do not know at this stage if I will ever witness this subatomic energy flow, this microcellular change, but I do know I see more clearly now what propels my actions.

If I leave with this alone, it is witness enough. Tomorrow is vipassana day. We will finally know what it is. I don't know how it can possibly be more than what I have already experienced. I hope I don't faint, or cry more, or see paranormal visions or something. I really hope it's not guns and a scramble for food in the deep mountains.

Actually, scratch that. I am so light, so unburdened, I am up for anything now. I even tap at my roomie's curtain to ask if I should switch off the light tonight.

Day 4

Others' Socks

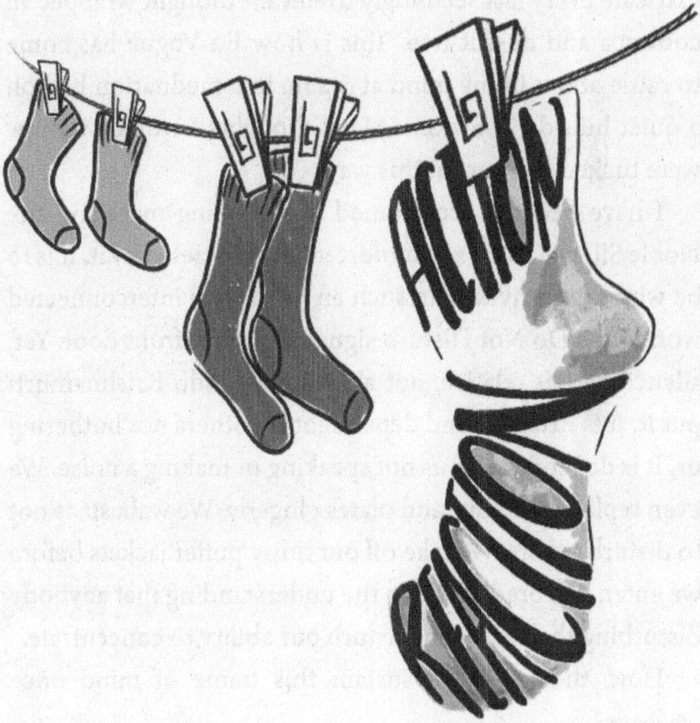

'FREE YOUR MIND AND THE REST WILL FOLLOW!' BY En Vogue screeches in my mind. I have not heard that song since I was a teenager watching MTV, so it startles me like a sharp whistle on a hungover morning. I assume the meditation goes into forgotten corners to extricate every last seemingly irrelevant thought wrapped in cobwebs and dust it free. This is how En Vogue has come to rattle about in my mind at 5 a.m. in a meditation hall on a quiet hillside in Sikkim. Many thoughts I wouldn't know were tucked away erupt this way.

I have become accustomed to wrapping myself in the Noble Silence like it's a comforter. I feel cosseted by it. It is to be worn as a privilege in such an intricately interconnected world, this Do Not Disturb sign hung at my front door. Yet, silence here is relative, not absolute as Jiddu Krishnamurti put it. It is external, and dependent on others not bothering us. It is dependent on us not speaking or making a noise. We even replace our cups and plates gingerly. We walk so as not to disturb others. We take off our noisy puffer jackets before we enter. It is predicated on the understanding that anybody disturbing the peace will disturb our ability to concentrate.

How, then, will we sustain this frame of mind once we leave?

True silence is that which emanates from inside out, not outside in. I set aside these concerns for now, grateful that I who don't know how to be silent from the inside at least have the external quiet for now. Luxuriating in it, the mind is becoming keener now. Every noise, from the twitter of a bird to the construction work going on down the hill, is heightened. At one point, I can hear a bee buzzing at the window. I have begun to hear a mild pulsing sound, and I don't know where it is coming from. I try to ignore it and focus on the Teacher's voice.

When I began this process, I found the Teacher's chants in Pali odd. I did not comprehend his words, and I found his voice a weird intrusion. His spoken voice in Hindi reminds me of Shashi Kapoor mouthing a film dialogue. He has the same polish of diction and linguistic swagger. Every time he offers an explanation, I find myself meditating on Shashi Kapoor's movies. What was that one with Leela Naidu where he goes off on a spiritual pursuit? When the Teacher initiates a session with the instruction to calm the mind, or goes into deeper meditative chants, he slips into an Amitabh Bachchan baritone. I am fascinated by the process of the guided meditation.

I once hosted two German children on an exchange programme, who wanted to learn yoga and who asked me why instructors in India insisted on talking throughout sessions. Instructors keep telling us to be alone with our thoughts, but they keep talking to us through our practised silence. Since it was pointed out, I have noticed that it is a surprisingly universal practice and a slightly annoying one if the instructor is not able to maintain the calm with his voice. It is quite an underrated skill that you don't value till it goes wrong; kind of like Envelopegate at the 2017 Oscars, the wrong host can really mess things up. Never undervalue the merit of a good guided meditation. It's all in the voice. This one comes with a Shashi Kapoor–Amitabh Bachchan double billing, and it is an acquired taste initially that morphs into one of those award-winning all-time-great classics.

I have begun to wait for the Teacher to break into his chants, suttas and his Hindi commentary and instructions.

Vānī to vaśa mein bhalī
vaśa mein bhalā śarīra
par jo mana vaśa mein kare
vahī saccā vīra

The morning chant goes:

Good to have mastery over speech,
good to have physical mastery,
but one who has mastery over the mind
is the true champion.

He seems to be inducing a state of tranquillity using his voice to set you up with vibrations of calm. This is not explicitly told to us, but I suspect it is so. If you believe in the Hindu principle of sound and its impact, you will recognize the significance and efficacy of this practice. The meditation hall is layered with vibrations, and it makes it easier to come to focus even when you have just returned from outside. I see now why Dechen asked me to return to the hall after my meltdown the other day.

The Teacher has also asked us to dissociate notions of other practices, other traditions, religious methodologies and ideologies when we enter into vipassana. I must reluctantly peel my mind away from this overanalysis that derives from other learnings, everything I have ever heard or contemplated, all the spiritual books I have ever read and the gurus I've heard speak. I submit myself to the process being taught to me in the here and the now, without questioning it. I have to remind myself of this often.

I will have to ask the assistant teacher about the pulsing in the noon question hour. It is getting louder. As I make my way to the hall for the post-breakfast session, Navya stops me just outside. 'Do you want me to lend you a pair of socks?' she asks in a loud whisper. Um ... what? I am instantly irritated. She thinks I haven't understood. 'I have many socks; I can lend you a pair,' she says, pointing to my feet. I look down at my socks. She assumes they are the same ones I came with because they are the same colour, while I have several similar pink pairs. (I got a discount deal on thermal-lined hiking socks at Decathlon.) I think about explaining it to her, but decide not to waste my words. She shouldn't be focusing on my socks anyway. I shake my head and move away to enter the hall. 'Don't feel bad…' I hear her say as I sit down, determined to put it aside and have a good session. I was in a pleasant place in the pre-dawn session today.

However, the brief interaction has set my thoughts to violently fluctuate now. I am amazed at how much impact such a brief encounter has. In this sealed-off environment, the tiny seed of irritation is amplified as though my boss just told me I'm not getting a raise. I recognize that I have no reason to be this agitated. It feels like a test. Let it go, I tell myself. Let it go. Don't react. Yet, all that my thoughts are doing is reacting. Why is she focusing on my socks? Why should I have to explain to her I have multiple pairs? Who put her in charge of others' laundry? Are my socks smelly? Oh god! I hope my socks are not smelly. It must be because of the heat I've been feeling. Maybe my feet have been sweating and I didn't notice. If I bent down to smell my toes now, do you think someone would notice? I certainly don't know what socks she or anyone else is wearing. It's not my business…I am here to meditate. It just goes to show that her focus is not inward but outward. In the real world, however, there are always going to be people who comment on your socks. Your socks, your clothes, your house, your car, your kid, your job... so, maybe the socks are a metaphor for life. Is this how I am going to react every time someone comes up with a bitchy little comment? Before I know it, the session has ended and I have successfully meditated for a whole hour upon my pink socks. I am livid. At myself more than at her, but at her also. What a waste of a session. I wasn't going to say anything, but now I simply must, no?

I indignantly grab Dechen and request her to ask Navya not to speak to me. I explain the circumstances. My meditations have been disturbed. As I say it, I can hear myself sound like a pompous prick. So I make excuses for myself. Concentration is fragile and hard-won. One sentence and the whole session is thrown out. As I say this, I am aware it speaks more to the fragility of my practice than the magnitude of the intrusion. Dechen promises to let her know, but explains to me that Navya is a doctor, it is her nature to check on others, develop some compassion. It takes me till the post-lunch session, an alarming six hours later, to lose the sense of having been disrupted.

I recognize that there is a massive kernel of ego sitting like an avocado stone in the core of my meditation. This is the same instinct that makes you want to be the first in class to put your hand up and answer when the teacher asks a question. The urge to know and to be seen as knowing, even if the knowledge is good, wholesome knowledge, is also driven by the ego. And ego comes from longing, clinging and craving for appreciation. It comes from needing to maintain a specific image we have built or seek to build of ourselves, I will later learn. The question hour is filled with students who want to be seen asking the right kind of questions, because this shows us to be sincere, intelligent, progressive aspirants. It is self-satisfying to be on the right track. I know. I know better than others. I am more sincere than others. I achieve results sooner than others. I am a concerned and eager student. Therefore, my practice is superior. Therefore, my practice is worthy of attention, protection. Therefore, I am more evolved. These are all superimpositions of the ego on the self that turn a course or class or session into a competition. In the moments where I recognize this, I realize that answers cannot be provided for me. A teacher can only push me back on the path when I veer off, but it is I who must observe and accept all that my mind is throwing at me. All of this, from pettiness to discovery, is all me.

I tell Dechen on the way to lunch that I have a question for the noon hour about the pulsing. 'When we are new, we bombard the assistant teacher with questions; when we have understood, we have no questions to ask,' she says. How ironic, I think. I have to pull myself back from self-aggrandizement and ask the question from the point of view of pure knowing. The pulsing is annoying me and it stops every time I exit the hall. I want to know where it's coming from.

They give us fruit custard to celebrate vipassana day, and I feel like a sacrificial lamb. What if there are strange goings-on at night? I glance at the steep hillside to the right and map it in case I need to make a run for it. Perhaps I should tuck away some salt from the dining hall in case I need to escape and fend off the leeches that they warned us infest the forest on the way.

Vipassana will be taught in the late afternoon session. We will be graduating from spiritual kindergarten. To think that all the realization I have come to so far I will think of as basic. But it doesn't feel basic to me right now. I remember a twelfth-standard psychology teacher who once laughed at the sight of us fighting with her for an extra half mark here and there. She said to us then, 'From where I am sitting, it looks like children crying that someone else got the bigger bar of chocolate. One day you will recognize what is trivial.' I don't care any more about how much I scored in psychology in college, but I do want to know what happens in the advanced vipassana courses. The sixty-day golden pagoda sessions in which meditators take to single cells for days on end. I recall meeting a Rajya Sabha MP who meditates in the tantric tradition (not the vipassana tradition). He has told me about demonic forces that attempt to disturb his meditations. I shudder. I think of a favourite Marathi abhang by Sant Tukaram, 'lahanpan dega deva' (God, keep me small), and think, maybe I should just stay small and do insignificant surface meditation. This much realization is enough for me. I don't even want to be a high-school graduate. It's only going to get tougher, I suspect. If so, what would motivate us to keep going?

So far, we have been allowed to change our positions. On the noticeboard is a sign that explains that after vipassana is taught, we will need to sit in aditthana, or with fierce determination, without moving our hands or legs or opening our eyes. We are required to come to physical and mental equanimity, the buzzword of the day. Nothing to it, just swim to equanimity island. I feel a panic rising, but I am trying to tread water. For now, I head to the hall armed with my highly intelligent question.

There are four segments of the mind – vinnana, sanna, vedana, sankhara – consciousness, perception, sensation and reaction. Four days of isolation and meditation have enhanced the sharpness of the whole mind. I seem to be overwhelmed by sanna. What I am hearing is the electromagnetic pulse of the loudspeakers when they are plugged in, I realize in the now nearly empty hall. Along with focus, the visual, audio, sensory inputs to the mind have also increased. That is why small aggressions seem much larger here than they would were they part of a normal day outside. I also probably wouldn't blow up at someone asking me about my socks in the regular course of a day. It is up to me, says the assistant teacher, to pull the focus of my mind away from these distractions and bring it back to the breath. There must be nothing but breath. The mind is still all over the place. I need to pull the focus from this broad reception and tune in to sensation on the body alone. Chastised, I resolve to try harder in the afternoon session.

The assistant teacher has been calling us to answer his questions about our progress in groups of three during the post-lunch sessions. One day it is old students, the next, novices. He asks us what we feel, whether we feel the sensation at the tip of the nose, whether we are able to sit longer now and whether we are able to focus on the breath. Then he worriedly makes notes in his notebook. It feels like school. Sometimes he suspects we answer according to what our neighbour says, like copycats. When he first came in, we thought he was elderly and possibly foggy, impatient with those of us who give rambling answers, but as the days go by, he is revealed to be keen and equipped with substantial expertise. He sees through the wishy-washy answers. He cuts short those who are simply talking to kill time. He is concise and correct. I like him immensely. We have discovered that he lives in Mumbai, down the road from me, near my parents' house. How about that? What's that they say about travelling all around the world for truths and finding them in your own backyard? We resolve to exchange contact information and keep in touch once the course ends. He also thinks we should all meditate for an hour each in the morning and the evening once we leave. Yeah, I will probably avoid him. Don't want to lie to my meditation teacher.

As we sit in the hall meditating, we cannot help but overhear the questions and problems others speak of. For Sita, who says she cannot feel anything, he advocates she stick to her reality and keep her focus. For Jessica, who has not made much progress and is consumed by her pain, he only has to gently scratch the surface for what ails her. It is her turn to share her outpouring of grief. No teacher can solve our problems, but they can help us recognize the blockages we each have that are preventing us from meditating. We recognize that we are all running, one way or another. We are all fragile in different ways. As some of us break down, those who haven't yet wonder why they haven't got there. No one's trauma is greater or more pressing than another's. All of us don't arrive at our truths in the same way. We will realize this much later, when the course ends. For now, we are still insecure about where we are. We just each get to where we need to be when it works for us. Our evolutions are ours alone.

I peep over at the male side of the congregation that I've so far managed to forget exists though they are in the same room, separated from the women by a narrow cloth runner on the floor. One of the fellows there is staring at Jessica. He seems unselfconsciously taken with her. She hasn't noticed. She has her eyes shut. Creep, I think to myself, feeling protective. I have no way to warn her. Just as well. Better not draw her attention to it and agitate her. That guy certainly needs to meditate, and I'm suddenly glad at least he's here and trying. I wish him well and turn away, reminding myself that to someone else watching me, I'm also looking across when I'm not supposed to. The man speaking with the assistant teacher is a BSF soldier, and I feel the urge to catch his eye and let him know I think he's very brave and I am glad someone who works such a tough job is taking some time out for self-care. I shut my eyes and send him good vibes. The men seem to sit down with extremely annoying, specific questions. 'Sir, it is going out and in, and then out instead of in, and out and then in.' 'Sir, when I sit down, my right leg crosses over my left shin and then my left ankle is left hurting, which impacts my back.' 'Sir, I am a physiotherapist by profession. What exercises do you recommend for such sustained and prolonged stresses on the limbs?' We reveal so much about ourselves, from our self-image to our intentions, through the questions we ask. I am not supposed to have noticed anything around me, least of all the men, but I think we are all listening quietly to each other under those tightly shut eyelids. Or maybe it's just me. Who knows?

The men never seem to burst into tears in emotional trauma during a meditation session, I notice. Hmpf, typical. I bet all our traumas, everything that has moved us women to tears variously, have some genesis somewhere in the actions of a man.

The session ends, and I take my break and go back to my thoughts. All our thoughts are locked into two categories: concerns either about the past or about the future. When we receive the vedanas, or sensations, our sankharas, or reactions, respond by falling under positive and negative categories. These are our aversions and cravings. The trick is a word that the Teacher repeats often: anicya, non-reaction, to either of them. This bestows equanimity. Today, I am swatting my cravings and aversions like my grandfather sitting on the front porch of his ground-floor flat in Matunga swatting flies with his buzzer bat.

I come to realize there is a commonality to Truth. In the works of Jiddu Krishnamurti, Ramana Maharshi, Swami Vivekananda, Sri Aurobindo, or Zen masters like Taigu Ryokan, Ikkyu Sojan and Matsuo Basho, modern masters like Thich Nhat Hanh and Eckhart Tolle, the insights into this exploration of the mind they offer are universal. Come to focus on the breath in the present. Befriend simplicity. Forgo the trappings of rites, rituals, traditions, religions. In silence you find non-differentiation and, in it, release. When you arrive at the kernel, it is all in the end the same path. The Teacher explains in the evening discourse what Gautama, the Buddha's distinct contribution has been. It has been accessible practice. It's a declassified map that gets you to your goal.

All the wise men keep telling you not to react, but how do you not react? As we have seen, even socks can be catastrophic to concentration if the mind so chooses. One way is to remove the stimuli. Monks, for instance, wear, consume and use minimally. You can reduce your consumption, but you can't eradicate it. No matter how determinedly you turn your face or exit the room from one antagonist or provocateur, there is no guarantee there will not be another elsewhere. Thus, you will spend your life running. (Ahem, Exhibit A here.) The second is to remove yourself. Suicide is not painful just for you but so much more for those you leave behind. If you believe in reincarnation and rebirth, you're going to have to deal with the pain you were attempting to escape from again in the next life, in another body, anyway. So it's pointless. You can't outrun or escape your lessons. For those who question afterlife or rebirth as speculative or as a myth, it is true we don't actually know anything about what comes after. For the here and the now, suicide is not an arriving at – it is a giving up, and giving up doesn't leave you with answers. I believe that if enlightenment exists, it must be freeing, it cannot be burdensome.

The third option the Buddha arrived at was by observing himself in response to what happens externally. Every time you are provoked, either to hate or to love, to joy or to pain, it is you who are responding with a corresponding craving or aversion. The response originates in your mind. It manifests through the body, the senses. All action, then, has its genesis in thought. Before you physically act or react, you have had a think about it. It takes some violence to act out of hate to a person. Let's say you strike him. Your thought will have puffed itself up to such violence with some full-scale bodybuilding. There is a substantial gap between thinking of hitting someone, saying you will hit them, and actually hitting them. Your thoughts of longing must build themselves up to manifest as actions of lust. There's a difference between thinking a stranger on the bus is pretty and going up to them and telling them so, or stroking their face. Most of us recognize this distinction when it comes to thoughts morality categorizes as 'wrong'. Perhaps it is training, but we tell ourselves not to think them, and if we think them, not to act on them. But we are unable to do this with, say, craving fast food that we spot in a shop window. Often, our actions follow our thoughts like slavish lambs. This is because we do not cultivate a rigorous training of not reacting. This distinction is what is achieved through meditation.

The simple solution, the Buddha discovered, is to cut off the action at the stage of thought. Separate the thought from the action. Take it a stage higher. Within the mind, cut off even the mental reaction from the arising thought and its corresponding sensation. That is, cut the sankhara off from the vedana. Let what may come at you, positive or negative. It's like muting trolls on Twitter. Let 'em rant. Let 'em praise. Do not react. Keep saying what you have to say. Pick your responses.

I wonder if Jack Dorsey came to the realization during his vipassana course that he had invented an endless sankhara machine. I'd have run out of the hall screaming at that point if I were him.

When you don't react to the stimuli, you dissipate the thought. Vipassana is the technique that breaks this link. As you witness the impermanence with clarity, you are introduced to your real self. When he arrived at this, Gautama, the Buddha sang, 'Gahakāraka! Diṭṭhosi, puna geham na kāhasi!' (Oh, householder! Now you are seen! You shall not build a house again for me!)

This is all very well said and sounds impressive in this 'Hear Yoda I do' kind of way, but try telling your legs that after ten hours of ardhapadmasana. Go on, I dare you. I have begun to talk to my feet now. 'I won't react to you,' I say to my crushed appendages, which refuse to acclimatize to this new regime. 'Come on, it isn't so hard. You were okay after those first few days at the gym, remember?' We are happy to acknowledge, amid our ice packs and hot-water bottles, that some (minimal) amount of pain meant we were doing it right. By the third day, our limbs are as enthusiastic as

anyone resolute with a hooked-by-the-offer annual membership. We have all been there. But here, there is no change. The discomfort is not growing on me, and I have worn stilettos in my lifetime. We are each in incredible pain. I overhear Diana tell the assistant teacher she has not been in such agony in all her life. I am starting to suspect the purpose of the meditation is to show us that if we create enough pain for ourselves, all our other material pains will pale in comparison. Right on! I get how this works now.

The vipassana teaching is given to us at 2 p.m. Maybe it is my imagination because we have been told it is a special teaching, but the Teacher's chants seem suffused with vibration and energy. Through the audio guidance, he moves our attention from the sensations on the nape of the nose to the top of the head. In the middle of the teaching my mind is searching for the word – is it fontanelle? I acutely feel the lack of Google to confirm that. It's okay, I make a mental note to look it up later. I have never been parted from a pencil and paper, or some medium by which to jot down notes or confirm information, before. I haven't even taken a holiday in which I did not write before. I find that more difficult to adjust to than the lack of phone calls or messages. I am quite sure people I love will survive without me. To write, jot, journal, however, is my perennial crutch. I am learning to walk without it, but it throws up one hell of an internal dialogue to compensate. The vipassana teaching courses energy down from the incompletely ossified top of the head, the primal seat of energy, especially in Hinduism, over every physical aspect of the body, down to the toes. This is a bit like *The Matrix*, flipping perfectly solid cells into fluctuating orbs of energy until we are nothing but a mass of subtle vibrations. As the mental scan moves downwards along with the Teacher's instructions, I feel a pulsing in my body. The cool burn of the too-much Vicks has spread as though my entire body has been dipped in a vat of the stuff. I am sweating profusely now, and can feel the trickles run down my neck, my back, my legs. We have been told not to move a finger except extremely slowly during the teaching, and so I don't know how to throw my shawl off. To be honest, I feel a little scared of the sensation. I want to open my eyes to know if this is normal, if this is what my co-meditators are experiencing. But the instruction has been so strict that I assume they assume I would not violate them. Who knows what realm of the subconscious I would find myself exiled to if I did? I keep my eyes tightly shut, like a child who has been told by elder siblings to not open them until she has counted to 100 or she will be 'it' in perpetuity. I obey. I find it laughable that I do, because I have been a singularly disobedient child all my life. Which is probably why I am here in the first place, in need of some spiritual assistance. Oh well. Is it only my mind that is wandering? Who knows?

At one point in aditthana, I am telling myself to remember giving birth. Think that you have a baby inside you and if you move abruptly, you will injure him, I say to myself. If you can do it for your son, you can do this for your spiritual birth, I'm cajoling my body. It actually feels worse, and I am on the brink of giving up and changing positions. I am now imagining a non-existent baby in my womb who needs to urgently come out. Aiyyaiyayay. I take a breath and begin again. Come on, the pain can't be that bad? Well, when they tell you that you are not supposed to move, all your mind is telling you is that if you don't move you will die.

Overeager to finish, my mind scans ahead of the instructions. I am at my stomach when he is still asking us to scan our arms. I've finished the last toe when he is asking us to start work on our legs. I am an impatient student. In some time, my mind is running the scan top to bottom, top to bottom, multiple times, imaging it to be a moving loop of light. Zoop zoop zoop. I feel giddy, as though I were on a looping slide. Okay, I'm done. I have vipassana-ed. Is this it, I want to ask.

Surely, we have been doing this for well over an hour, I think. Maybe they forgot to switch on the timer to let us know when we're done. I peek a little. Everyone else seems to be deeply focused. Exhilarated by my little cheat, I shut my eyes again. I wait a little to see what happens. I am not blasted to the nether lands. I take a chance and toss my shawl off my arms. Phew. I needed that.

My mind chastises me. I am here to learn, not prove myself superior. The aim of taking the course was to confer on myself some calm, a meditative state of mind, not win a jamboree and go home with a medal. I must do what I can do and if I can't, well, I can't. I shut down the scan and go back to listening to what the Teacher is saying in his audio instruction. 'From head to toe, scan each and every part of your body, leave nothing out,' he is saying. I need to be more deliberate. I go back and concentrate on the pulse at the centre of the top of my head. Where even is my fontanelle, I wonder. What if I have assumed its position when it's actually ten centimetres to the left? Are we allowed to lift up our hands and feel for the centre? What if my mind has found a centre that is not my body's centre? Do those misalignments ever happen? For now I'll work with a guesstimate. I go where the pulse is strongest. It feels like a beam of light shining out of a torch off the top of my head. I wonder if someone more advanced in meditation can actually see it. Does it ever close up, now that we have been initiated? Or do we initiates now walk around with beams of light shooting out of our heads?

I am not being flippant. Okay, maybe a little bit. Everyone takes the spiritual growth thing so seriously. As though our lives depended on it. Well, they do, all of our many lives, but if we're doing it right, we should lighten up. We have probably done much worse things than have a sense of humour, so I don't think having one is going to send me by default into another rebirth. One of the things that draws me to this Teacher in particular is that he has a wicked and deadpan sense of humour. He is unpretentious and simple, which makes me trust his teaching a little more. While discussing the image of god that man has framed, he wonders what kind of god he would have to be if he insisted all his followers chanted his name to show their devotion to his teachings. 'Hey Goenka! Hey Goenka!' he mocks himself, doing a funny little dance to mock such misplaced self-aggrandizement. I think of him dancing and want to burst into laughter now. Good spiritual practice has to make us lighter, less susceptible to offence, and deflate the ego, not make us more self-important and self-righteous. He mocks the people who donate to charity and then plaster hospitals and schools with their names. He offers his own name as example: Goenka Hospital, Goenka School, Goenka College, Goenka Airport. If Goenka was truly an enlightened soul, it wouldn't matter to him. Why do we erect such false gods? Why do we not see through them? If our efforts don't leave us with these visible outcomes of enlightenment, we're probably doing it wrong. The Teacher is great not because he is a funny man, but because he pokes holes in our self-importance, and makes the false nature of the self we have built fall away. He makes it look so easy, but if we have learnt anything from the Buddha, it is that the most sublime truths are the simplest. In light of them, falsehoods seem so ridiculous as to be funny. This is the nature of lightness.

Ryokan sang,

You must rise above
the gloomy clouds
covering the mountaintop
otherwise, how will you
ever see the brightness?

(*Lust for Enlightenment*, tr. John Stevens)

Vipassana works not merely because it is a technique that takes you into the layers of your mind and body, but because it is accessible. Gautama, the Buddha was not the first buddha, the teacher reminds us. There were buddhas before him and there will be buddhas after him. Because everyone can, and many do, attain the same state of enlightenment if they do the work. The system cannot presume to mark anyone's progress or state of evolution – only you can do that for yourself – and if it works, you see the results in yourself. You become free of anger, resentment, ego. You release the angst. Your struggle separates from the sides of the pan like tomato passata cooked through. You're done. You may serve and be served. I am suppressing my laughter now in this hall of very serious meditators. I know I am in the right place when I feel the laughter course through me, like a child giggling at a hopelessly silly joke once again. I feel it vibrate in my core, melding into a long-forgotten resonance of how carefree life once used to be. You remember? Before we began to think about what people thought of us. Wearing shopping bags as spacesuits and parading around the house with paper swords. When Tom and Jerry made us double up with laughter, and Abbott and Costello was the funniest thing on TV. I feel my shoulders gently shake with suppressed convulsions. I remember that this is what I came here for. I am laughing again.

I forget to open my eyes when the closing gong sounds, and this time when the tears come, the hall is emptying itself out and these are the residue of too much good feeling. I know the Teacher said don't react, even with joy to sensations that make you feel happy, but I allow myself this one. There is an extra layer of depth to the silence at tea. You can hear the muri crunching. Dechen, who keeps an extra cup of tea for me in the jug, asks why I have not been taking seconds of anything, at lunch or at tea. Am I feeling okay? Am I unwell? I haven't noticed that I don't need it any more. Food has become functional, and I have begun to eat when I have to, and I do not think about it so much at all. Dinner is a houseguest that has finally got the hint that he has overstayed his welcome.

The sutta for Day 4 is from the Buddha Jayamangala Aṭṭhagāthā, suttas sung to celebrate the Buddha's victory and to protect oneself during meditation in the Theravada tradition. They narrate a series of stories that outline the obstacles he had to overcome, from demons to mad elephants lunging at him, and embarrassing attempts at character assassination by foes, to triumph over his mind through vipassana. That old Hindi song comes to mind: 'Kuchh reet jagat ki aisi hai har ek subah ki shaam hui, Tu kaun hai tera naam hai kya Sita bhi yahan badnam hui...' (The ritual of life is such that every morning must descend into dusk. Who are you? What's your name? Even Sita was besmirched here...) They tell us the Buddha achieved his nirvana on a full-moon night. The last night of our course will coincide with the full moon of Holi. It feels like an auspicious sign.

I have lived in an ashram environment before and know from experience that one criticism people like to level is that inmates or practitioners of spiritual techniques are not saintly. Well, if they were saintly, they wouldn't need the practice, right? It's all of us, who've done terrible things in our own ways, hurt people around us, made irresponsible choices, who need a little help. Religious institutions and spiritual environments everywhere are microcosms of the larger outside world. They are also replete with politics, bad deeds, difficult people and questionable actions. At best, we come here with the understanding that we are flawed, and that we need to rectify ourselves, which is a start.

> Ukkhitta khaggamatihattha-sudāruṇantaṃ
> dhāvanti yojanapath-angulimālavantaṃ;
> iddhibhisankhatamano jitavā munindo
> tam tejasā bhavatu tam the jayamangālani
>
> With upraised sword in his hand, implacable,
> Angulimala pursued him for one yojana.
> With a mind prepared by psychic powers, the Lord of Sages conquered him.
> By the power of such virtues, may victory and happiness be yours.

The Teacher's chant tells the story of the Buddha's encounter with Angulimala, the dacoit-turned-saint. It is a story I have heard before. I think despite my misdeeds, maybe I am not beyond redemption. In his explanatory discourse later in the evening, the Teacher describes how Angulimala, now transformed into a monk, goes out to preach dhamma. Several villagers who recognize him as a former dacoit abuse him and reject his insights. He persists. They throw stones at him, beat him up, toss him out of the village limits. It is a curious story that many of us have limited to inspiration for transformation alone.

When we set ourselves about our transformation, we also do so tired of criticism, brickbats, obstacles and the lack of success. In my understanding, where I once saw them as punishments, I see them now as markers that show us we need to course-correct. When something is right, it flows through. When something is wrong, we will know, we will be told. We hope that when our process of transformation is done, when we have arrived at this new us, miraculously, circumstances and people will treat us better. Religious institutions in this country are filled with rows of congregants hanging on hope of such transformation. Spas, life coaches, motivational programmes and rehab centres survive by offering hope of such turnarounds. We believe there ought to be a reward for transformation. If a no-good fellow transforms silently in the forest, and nobody sees it or is impacted by it, is he transformed at all? We expect recompense for our goodness, universal acceptance and applause for our endeavours. I who have done wrong am now good. I have gone from point A to point B and the view must change as a result of my journey. My environment will be transformed, my obstacles will disappear, and the success and outcomes I want to see will manifest. They probably will, but not for the reasons we think they will. Perhaps Angulimala's story is a lesson that, while I am not too far gone, adopting the vipassana technique doesn't mean my problems or critics and antagonists will go away. I'll just stop reacting to them.

In the few split seconds during meditation in which I am able to not react to what my thoughts throw up at me, or to itch the scratches my body summons, I know how liberating it is not to be at anyone's beck and call. The criticism may come, the obstacles may come, the stone-pelting may come. I am no longer obliged to respond. My actions do not have to be contingent on others' response to them. I have no expectation of others' response to them, whether they be positive or negative towards me. So how does it matter then? When expectation falls away, action in itself becomes self-contained and self-fulfilling.

I will do me. You will do you. In this practice, we are all set free to be ourselves. Thank you, Angulimala.

My roomie taps the door. I don't respond. I don't get irritated. I consider for a minute giving her an answer, but realize I am not obliged to. She taps because it is in her nature to. I don't reply because it is not my need to. We are both set free by separating our action and reaction.

Day 5

The Purpose of Pain

I have never quite felt so grateful to shiver at the bitter cold again. The heat has gone away. I have been awake since 3 a.m., huddling under my fleece blanket, staring at the wooden roof, waiting for the bells to go off. My breath emerges in cold puffs, hanging in the air after I have passed on my way to the hall. As soon as I seat myself, the cool burn of the menthol-infused sensation courses through my body as if on cue. It flows into every nook and cranny, consuming it to the point of no distinction. I feel like a dynamo, capable of producing enough electricity to power a small village. Up and down the energy flows, giving me a rocker of a session. At one point, I feel myself distinct from my body, watching it, the pain in my forelimbs distant and underlying. It feels invigorating, awake, elevated. I gloat in the feel-good. Ah, this is what it feels like to be one with oneself, I think.

The amount of rubbish we are willing to believe of ourselves is directly proportional to the number of poorly researched self-help articles we read in waiting rooms of salons. We have read so much about what enlightenment is supposed to feel like that if the Buddha himself came to us with a teaching that showed us otherwise, we would reject it as not liberating enough. The morning meditation is so textbook perfect – energizing, filling me with positivity, feeling charged, come to stillness – all the buzzwords of the meditation industry fill me up to bursting point. I am swelling up with a smug sense of achievement. I feel so happy in the embrace of this sensation that something feels off. How do I even know if anything I am feeling is real? Nothing is sitting right. Even the sight of Little Buddha, stoic in her all-purple tracksuit does not uplift me today.

The sugar rush crashes shortly after breakfast. A bleakness descends, and not merely because the sky is overcast. I am tossed into a state of doubt. The sutta for the day is a hark back to organized religion.

Gangā Jamunā Sarasvati
sīla samadhi jñāna
tīnoṅ kā saṅgam hove
pragaṭe pada niravāṇa

The true Ganges, Jamuna and Sarasvati
are morality, concentration and wisdom.
Where these three streams converge,
nirvana manifests.

It's a message I've heard so many times it feels redundant. So what's new? Blah blah everybody needs to be morally upright. What is moral for one is immoral for another. One way of prayer and meditation is superior to another. This teacher has the answers, that one is a fraud. Cue all the moral policing and communal rioting in the world. Been there, seen that. So why is the Teacher telling us that vipassana has nothing to do with religion? We may not be following established mantras, but we are following other suttas, stories and methodologies. We may not bow to gurus, saints and gods, but we are following another master and idolizing him without question, bowing to television sets, to chants of words we don't actually understand. We may not be intellectualizing received wisdom, but we are taking the Teacher's words on faith. We could be anywhere and doing the same thing. The reason why vipassana has taken off to the extent that it is now a celebrity fad is because it is organized as an accessible network of courses you can graduate through to a hierarchy of self-discovery. Organized religion by any other name, with the order rearranged to incorporate disbelief, is still religion. I wonder if I am enlisted into just another cult, as my atheist son labels all my spiritual endeavours.

Doubt is a process of elimination integral to arriving at the truth. Any teaching that advocates a lack of questions is a dubious one. As I meditate further, I find that doubt periodically erupts to shake the foundations and to allow the fragile to fall away. The suspicious mind, like the monkey mind, serves a purpose. Today, I am falling out of the sky without a parachute, landing with a thud and a smack that leaves a terrible ache in my bones.

The technique of vipassana has thrown open the doors to a world of pain. As my mind scans each inch of my body, every hidden bit of pain is brought to the fore. I find the sitting exhausting now. I don't see the point of creating pain for ourselves and then claiming not to react to it. If all sensations create cravings and aversions, why don't we make a practice of not reacting to the cravings? By all means make us sit in front of a large chocolate cake and tell us not to eat it. It would be far more pleasant than this. Or how about playing some nice music and telling us not to sway and dance or feel joy? That way, when we fail, my failure will entail eating cake and dancing. We fail pleasantly. Why only pain? Eckhart Tolle in *The Power of Now* speaks of the dangers of carrying an identifiable pain body around. When we nurture that sense of being wounded, we cultivate it, we dwell in it. When something goes wrong in the morning and you've decided you're now going to have a bad day, you are consumed by the negative and drag it along with you through your day. Your mind is so weaned towards the negative that it is all you can see. We all know people like that: no matter what they have, they are miserable. No matter how little I have had, I have always been happy. Yes, I am smug about what keeps me ticking. It makes me feel good. I like joy. I truly do. This feels like a poor trade-off. I don't see why I should enter into it.

This way of living, I fear, confers a pessimistic bent of mind. The premise of the spiritual quest is that life is suffering and it urges you to recategorize your life in terms of all the pain you have suffered. But is life truly entirely suffering? I have lived a very fulfilling life. I've had a great childhood – I grew up in Africa, licking gari and chicken stew off my fingers, holidayed at the Kilimanjaro and across Europe, moved to the beautiful hill town of Kodai, went to school by ferry across a lake and then on a horse uphill, had wonderful friendships and relationships with good men and women. Moving often made me flexible and adaptable to life and circumstance. So much good in my life has more than compensated for the bad. I have met kind strangers out of the blue who became family. Good people are to be found everywhere – on flights, in trains, a hotel in some corner of the world.

My son and I have almost grown up together, as I had him when I was twenty-four, barely knowing what I was doing, and we share a special bond because of the escapades we've been through together. I am proud that he has taken the best of me and become his own person. I take credit for the seed of good in him. I've done well at work and the obstacles taught me resilience and how to get back on my feet, remain ethical and become self-sufficient. I have what I need, and what I don't have I do not need. I have few health issues and the means to treat them. I have travelled, eaten, read, written, shared well and well enough to fill my heart with good memories that I am going to think of when my son puts me in that home. I have nothing to complain about. From a lot of seemingly awful things, good things emerge, foils to enhance the good. Why should I define my life by them alone?

I take a walkabout and stop to look at the cloud-obscured mountain range. You cannot but feel its might. Even partially cloaked, the Himalayas are awe-inspiring. I feel blessed to be born into a country that has this by way of natural beauty at its borders, alongside the crazy chaos that is Mumbai or the quiet coconut groves along the backwaters of Kerala. Who gets this much? No wonder people come here from all over the world to seek recharge and direction. We are bounteous as a culture. We are inherently a tolerant people. You have to be particularly negative not to appreciate all that you have. I have seen several good minds destroyed by their inability to count their blessings. Positivity is not thinking all will be well when it clearly isn't – it is seeing that whatever comes your way brings some good with it. As Jiddu Krishnamurti put it, my secret is I don't mind what happens. It's always a thrill to me to see how low the low can go and how high the high. It is bleak to sit in a cavernous room and refuse to take in the once-in-a-lifetime view and insist that life is suffering. What kind of masochism is that?

I seriously wonder for the first time if I should leave. I do not want to break down the strength of my mind with this all-encompassing pessimism. If I disagree with the premise, what is the point of continuing with the practice?

I don't want to damage myself by slipping into a negative way of thinking. It can undo years of positive focus in one shot. That positivity is integral to keeping me going. What if this breaks me down and I lose the will to carry on? I can't afford, quite literally, depression. I am scared to continue the practice now.

A second aspect of this focus on pain bothers me. Why are only the recipients of pain asked to think of perpetrators with compassion? Why do people who spend their lives wilfully injuring others get to lead seemingly successful lives? They don't seem to suffer material retribution, while those they inflict themselves upon end up broken in confidence, resolve and the ability to move on. How does not reacting to the bad help? Where there is evil, it must be acted against or it will continue unabated. We know this from history and the circumstances that surround us. I don't want to sit here and make excuses for the wrongdoers of the world. There are paedophiles and rapists and murderers and lynchers and embezzlers and wife-beaters around. I question why I should have compassion for any of them. My mind hits peak sulk and I'm not even trying this morning.

The assistant teacher has been asking meditators whether we feel the same sensation or different ones all over the body, nodding before he makes notes in his teaching diary. 'Different,' the meditators answer. Listening to the responses of the first few novices, I assume that maybe everyone feels this differently. Then I realize I'm probably the only one feeling a unitary homogenous sensation. I go to the assistant teacher in the noon question hour and ask him about it. He smiles. 'No, you shouldn't be feeling one sensation because your body carries the pain of different actions and reactions. They are not all the same. Your mind is projecting your feelings on to your body,' he says. I must correct course.

I realize I am doing it wrong. I have predefined what I ought to feel and I am telling my body to feel it. That is why it is not sitting right. Though it's freezing now, I decide to head for a bath to reset my body and the way it's carrying sensations. I do not have any shampoo, so I decide to wash my hair using my body wash. I stand in the cold and wait for the geyser to heat up again and fill my bucket twice. When I scrub my head, I try to push this malaise out of myself and perk up. The bath has been inducted into the spiritual process as a revitalizing function. Most of us do not need our post-lunch naps any more. The weather here is frequently mutable and flips in an instant, so we try to sit around in the sun or walk up and down to exercise our legs when we can. We are not actively avoiding each other as much, and if one of us catches the other's eye, we do acknowledge it and let it pass. As I sit in the sun to dry my hair, I decide to try again in the afternoon sessions.

I have learnt that the trick to meditating is not to try harder; it is to stop trying and step back. It sounds paradoxical, but it is not. When I stop trying to focus, what is blocking the free passage of the mind has space to emerge and dissipate.

I am not giving the technique a fair chance by disallowing its premise. I am fighting my doubts right now. That won't work. If I have to get past this, I must allow my questions to rise. I must acknowledge that I have them and feel this way. I cannot proceed unless I deal with the reality of how I feel.

I feel an anger at those I carry an aversion to. Why do I love or hate? I think about a former colleague whose dealings I could not go along with. I was threatened with dire consequences if I stood in his way. I complained, naively believing in the system, but found no support. Left with no choice, I stormed out of the job. At the time, I had a four-year-old to look after on my own. I spent the next six months in debt, pleading for jobs everywhere. Systematic character assassination followed. Jerked around while trying to make a living, I felt harassed, humiliated and defeated. I agreed to an arranged match as an outcome of feeling completely beaten down. The gentleman in question had met the material checklist in my head, but all that quickly descended into behaviour and demands that my feminist core balked at. It spurred me to ask myself why I was being so uncharacteristically submissive to a way of life – a dependent spouse of an NRI – that held no attraction for me. I was not only escaping a bad situation through a door that would clearly lead to worse, I was also doing it in the hope of a social redemption I myself found scornful. We called the wedding off, and looking back, I thank my instincts. Over time, I have understood that my reactions have helped me escape abusive situations. I am immensely capable of seeing the silver lining in situations, even the worst of them.

However, it is hard for me to think of people like this and tell myself they don't matter. I do see some people as capable of immense evil. The damage they cause is personal, professional, economic and social. I remember crying in the bathroom when I was in that job, feeling the walls closing in around me. I needed the money; I didn't need the harassment. I didn't know what to do. Nothing in my life had prepared me for people who behaved this way. I had lived a fairly sheltered childhood. I slipped into depression. I know of others who have dealt with physical abuse, economic isolation, professional bullying, social boycotts and cruelty in many forms that have tangible repercussions on its victims. To put it mildly, I would like to see the effigies of some of these perpetrators burned in a parade at least once a year, and have governments declare that day a national holiday of celebration and a quasi-religion. I don't think I am acing this non-reaction thing. I am now breathing deeply and intentionally to calm myself. It is not working.

When we say release the past, think of those who have affected us with compassion, we are thinking of people who have wilfully forced us into situations of compromise and real pain. Just how dispassionate and compassionate can we really be? It's easy to talk, but how do we do it, even if we somehow motivate ourselves to do so?

Compassion is a widespread arriving at. I realize that you cannot have it for some and not for others. It doesn't work that way. The truly compassionate expend this energy towards everyone who crosses their path. I know because I have met people like that. It is a serene state of mind, not a basket of apples you choose to hand out to people you like. How do you extend it to the people who have harmed you or others? Missteps I understand – everyone makes mistakes, even those that cost you heavily. We all act foolishly and hurt the people we love sometimes, and are unmindful of the consequences. The Catholics distinguish between sins of omission and sins of commission. This is something like that. But those who knowingly push people to the brink of ruin, death, unemployment and displacement? What compassion are you suggesting I have for them? Why am I obliged to? I don't know when I have begun doing it, but at some point during the day, I realize, I have begun to have direct conversations with the Teacher in my head now. Try and tell me you're not leading a religion now, Guruji. I guess it is because I am too impatient to wait for the night's discourse. Some answers now would be nice, I think, offering him a shortcut.

compassion

I am taking more walkabouts today to relieve my anxiety. I buy some moments to myself each time I return to my seat by rearranging my cushions multiple times. I smooth and pat down the covers and fluff up the foam. We are all siphoning these little hacks from each other wherever we can find them, delaying our submission to the posture by stealing away microseconds. All except the Little Buddha. Only once has she swerved from her Noble Silence and that was when she ran into me on the porch as she was coming out of her room. She sits next to me in the hall and, clearly, I am more agitated than I have noticed because she must have felt my disturbed state of mind, though we are each sitting in perfect silence. All this upheaval is in my head alone. I am stunned at her ability to perceive it. 'Are you okay?' she had asked then, her lips exaggerating the vowels into 'O's without actually saying the words. I nodded to reassure her. Satisfied, she made her way to the hall, looking down.

I feel guilty to have been the cause of her concern. Our irritation at attempts to communicate in whatever way we are able to is much reduced now, because we each realize that if we don't, our meditation hours are entangled with thoughts about each other, which can be just as annoying. Over here, every small gesture, or lack of, is magnified. It's like sneezing in a capsule in outer space. It'll probably reverberate for light years until another expedition finds its residue. Our gestures linger like that in our meditative cones of silence.

I do viscerally feel hatred for some people because of what I have been put through on account of their actions. Contrarily, I have built up a sense of love for those who supported me. I do base my choices of work and friendship on these loyalties and aversions. To a lesser or greater degree, we all base our life directions on the affinities and repulsions we develop. So how do we not react in this way, and why should we not?

The voice of the Teacher is singing his chants over a recording, and I try to find some direction in them.

Jaisī cita kī cetanā
vaisa hī phala hoya
duramana kā phala dukhada hī
sukhada sumana kā hoy

As is the volition of the mind,
such will be the fruit,
an impure mind yields fruits of misery,
a pure mind yields happiness.

As we sow, so shall we reap. I must ask myself again what my culpability in these actions is. Have I not acted and reacted equally in someone else's perspective? If I have compassion for myself, knowing the chain in which I am caught, do I not owe that to others too?

What is the purpose of compassion? It is not completely altruistic, as we noted earlier. It frees us from reacting in precise, deliberate ways. Forgotten facts piece together. I know a friend who has been bad-mouthing me for years is caught in her own cycle of misery. Her anger is directed at my having everything so easily that comes to her with such difficulty. I see how trapped she feels. In her powerlessness, I become a symbol she can punish for her grief.

I realize her anger has little to do with me.

If we begin to consider the actions and circumstances of others with compassion, we will find the chain of action and reaction repeats. We will find that the actions that come from these are not personal, though they seem to be. We will find ourselves freed from needing to react. All the years of building up smart and wounding retorts, fantasizing about a justifiable revenge, fall away in an instant of understanding. I feel like I want to hug her – her pain must be so unimaginable. I couldn't be harsh to her now if I tried. I am brought to tears – this time, not for what she has done to me, but for what she is going through that I have not understood, even if she doesn't want or need my understanding. Within the span of a few moments, someone I considered an enemy for a long time is transformed into an object of compassion. I am released from my own pain about the situation. I no longer have to carry that once-inflicted wound around. People seek miracles, but it seems to me now that there is nothing more miraculous than the transformation of interpersonal relationships, the battleground of war and tragic longing alike. If I ran into her somewhere, I could very easily smile at her with compassion.

In the discourse later in the day, the Teacher will explain how what comes to us, comes to fulfil the sankharas of the past, in this life and previous ones. The people whom we confront are mere instruments of action. If not him, another. If not her, another. I will get the actions to my reactions that I have sown in the past. I cannot avoid them. Until I release myself from my reactions in the now, I will continue to have to confront reactions to my actions in the future. The solution is in the now. The solution is only in finding the compassion for each and every instance, no matter how difficult.

I am forced to confront each of these loves and hates now in my meditation. Little about this is the warm fuzzy self-actualization that meditation retreats advertise, replete with frangipani flowers, smart water, mountain mists and aromatherapy massages spawning a bill in lakhs. This one is free and microcellular-ly painful. I should have sold a kidney and gone to Ananda in the Himalayas, where I could be sipping green tea with Oprah.

I allow the faces and words of Enemy No. 1 (2, 3, etc.) to rise from the depths of my memory where I have buried them for a long time now. I refuse to feel anger, or fear. Of course, despite my determination, these emotions do arise. I let them. They linger like dark clouds. Each hovers as though waiting to see if I will grab its seeds and plant them, water them and allow them to multiply, manifest. I recognize that what they want is a reaction now. Some ranting will only inflate them more. I don't. I don't do anything. Emotions want attention. So they puff out their chests and make themselves seem bigger than they are. They throw tantrums. I let each expend itself like a thundercloud that needs to rain itself out. I watch until each fades away across that last ridge, becoming a rapidly diminishing speck. Sometimes I do catch myself adding more furious thoughts. Anger is also necessary, I think. At least now I am able to watch myself do so with some dispassion. It is no longer a rage that fills me or has the potential to sully my waters for hours together. The meditation has inserted layers of separation between me, my anger and the object of my anger. When rage and grief dissipate, I am able to bring my mind back to the object of the hate, the perpetrator, be it a boss or an ex, and contemplate him or her. If I have allowed the emotion to thunder itself into nothingness, I feel nothing now. If there is some residue, I repeat the process until I come to a null point again. Now, I can consider their motivations, where they came from, why they made me the object of vendetta and what outcomes it had for them. If I am overwhelmed by a sense of victimhood or self-pity, I allow the emotion to rain itself out, dissipate, and I begin again. This occurs multiple times. By the time I finish, they seem to be more a figure of pathos and tragedy than an object of anger. I feel silly for how much power I gave the antagonist to direct my course of actions.

More importantly, I am able to look past them and see, with clarity, myself in those roles. The practice has taught me to question the events of my life in reverse. When something has had a dissatisfactory outcome, I am able to ask myself if I got there for the wrong reasons. I have to ask myself how I came to know or aggravate an antagonist. How did I come to take that job? Was it a role I really wanted to be in or was I merely seeking an escape from the job I was in before it? Why did I put myself in such vulnerable positions? Why did I react with rage? Could I not have sought better resolution? What resulted from those reactions that I could have made better choices about? Where earlier I would have reacted with ego to this line of self-questioning, I am able to consider more objectively my own role. This is neither self-flagellation nor am I absolving the other. This is what is.

Time and again, with one suppressed memory or repressed emotion emerging after another, the clarity of how events unfold is proven repeatedly. Yes, people you encounter occasionally are wrong, do wrong. You cannot control them. You can only control your reaction to them. When you react for the wrong reasons, you will always do so in the wrong way. The outcome is never satisfactory, and will lead to another thread of cause and effect that you will keep adjusting to. I can keep blaming others for those consequences or recognize my own culpability in propagating the unending link.

If I had acted calmly, without anger, things probably would have probably ended differently. So, why did I react with anger? Because in a previous encounter with an uncomfortable situation, I didn't react with anger, and I was blamed for encouraging it. So the anger I carried was residual, reactive and disproportionate to the outcome. This job was an exit strategy to another uncomfortable situation, not a job I wanted or aspired to in itself, and thus was not a good fit for me. I would have left anyway. I wasn't seeking the boss's approval, and he sensed that. This added to my inability to be a boss's 'person' in the hot seat. This made me non-pliable, and him determined to evict me from the role. His own chain probably has its own endless permutations of motivations that are for him to analyse. He had bragged about replacing the previous incumbent when he took the job and was under pressure to fulfil them. He needed to prove himself. It was not personal, I was just in his way... yada yada yada. Our antagonists become instruments of their reactions, as do we. Suffice to say, so on and so forth, backwards and forwards, we sow the seeds of our actions and the outcomes of our reactions.

As we watch the Teacher's discourse, we hear a commotion outside the room. A young man has had an emotional breakdown, is in tears and has started shouting at the assistant teacher and the sevak to be allowed to go home. The agitated voice booming through the still night air startles us. All I know of him is that he is from Gurgaon, he shouts with a booming voice and he needed a chair because of an old leg injury. He has realized in his meditations that he has wronged his mother, and he wants to go back and make amends. The assistant teacher and the sevak plead with him to stay at least until the morning. It is pitch dark and past 8 p.m. on the isolated mountain ridge. It is bitterly cold, and rain is imminent. He won't listen to reason. He has to go see her, talk to her now. We shut the door to be able to focus on the discourse, and I don't know when he left, but when I turn to look for his chair in the morning, he won't be there. I will hope he resolves the conflict with his mother and the immense pain he seems to be carrying.

The sugarcane and the neem tree both emerge from the seed that is planted. With the same soil, watering, care, one will be bitter and the other sweet. When we look around and see people 'doing well', what we mean is they have money, designation, maybe enjoy respect and adulation, are thought of well, and seem to have the material things that we aspire to. We don't have access to them, so we think we have failed. Or worse, that we are being punished somehow. Thus, we equate comfort with good, lack of comfort with bad. We want the good, we don't want the bad. Duh, a no-brainer, you would think. The followers of the Buddha are like, 'No, dude, don't want good and don't want bad either.' Um, what? Why?

We grow up believing good = reward; bad = punishment. We take to prayer, meditation, remedies and transformations to improve our chances of gaining these material outcomes. We make religion, transformation, spirituality a votes-for-cash scheme. Do this for me, and I will get you what you want. It's a graft racket. You're not going to make your offering till the results are on the table, as the Teacher puts it. We operate like gangsters.

What if you were told that no amount of prayer or supplication would change your outcomes? Bring you what you want? Would you still pray? Ha, you think, but I've seen that it works. When I prayed, I passed that exam. When I made the offering, the other bidder mysteriously dropped out and I won the claim at an impossible price. When no medicine worked, offerings cured my relative. And when I am down, prayer lifts me up.

You cannot know these. They seem connected, so we assume they must be so. If we had to whittle down to what we actually see, feel and therefore know, we will have to eliminate these miraculous outcomes. Vipassana is about what you feel and know in the immediacy of your mind.

Prayer is calming to the mind, and when I am agitated, rhythmic chanting or meditation quietens it. Our minds work better when we are calmer. That's pretty much all I can say with certainty. Then what is the point of meditation at all? I am not going to miraculously get a high-paying job, see all my stocks zoom up, make lucky punts, move to a penthouse in New York, win an Oscar, marry a gazillionaire or dine with presidents. Then why do it? Probably nothing will change. Except me. Nothing will change but me.

I will change. That's all that I can change. I control nothing else. No earth or heaven will be moved for me. Opportunities will not come knocking at my door. I will not be suddenly and spontaneously loved. Bad things will happen, alongside the good. I will still be besieged by illness, provoked by antagonists, be manipulated by those in power, heckled by critics. If nothing changes, what changes?

Me. I change.

Where there was only pain in my legs, a day of vipassana practice has unleashed a differentiated pain in each and every cell of my body. Where my ankles throbbed, now I feel a burn in my toes, an ache in my sole, a crushing in my bones where the legs interlock. A pain of ages sears my lower abdomen, where it hugs my womb, my stomach carries a dull heaviness, my breasts feel pinched, my chest carries a sharp pain like a knife wound, my back is sore in spots, I feel internal twangs like a guitar with snapped strings, my nose continues to burn and my forehead, I realize, has several bands running through it like the one that snapped the other day when I cried.

Oh my god. There is such a long way to go. None of this is going to be released today.

What is the point of making me aware of each of these aches? I was perfectly fine simply walking around with a numb mind because I have had enough pain in my life. I don't need more. None of us needs more. I am overwhelmed by the fear that when I leave here, each of these pains will remain activated and I will forever walk around in excruciating pain.

I was better off burying my pain. If we remember every bit of pain, how can we move on? How can we forget? How can we forgive?

I used to think poor memory is the basis of a positive mind. The monkey mind loses its focus on pain too. Anicya

anicya anicya. Nothing is permanent. But there is equanimity from ignorance and equanimity from knowing.

nothing is permanent

We focus on pain to release it. As the Teacher put it in the evening's discourse, spot on as usual, when you see a man running at you with gasoline, you don't run at him with gasoline – common sense dictates you run towards him with water. When I do so, even just in my mind, the temperature cools just a bit. The reactions that lock me into persistent conflagrations fall away. I thought someday I'd say this and do that, and he would reply thus, and I'd have the perfect repartee, jab and thrust, and put it all in its place, and this matter would end with me triumphant. It ends here. This is it. There is no need to tell my story. At least five books I plan to write can now be shelved. There is no need to assuage myself. There is no revenge to be sought. There is no forgiveness to be meted out. There is no need for closure. I will not walk a step further with the perfect repartee stored away. There is nothing more. It is over. I am done doing battle.

I feel a deep silence reverberate over me. It feels like someone finally pulled the plug out of whatever machine I was hooked to. Like the pulsing of the speakers that finally fell away, I realize only when it stops that this reactiveness has been throbbing in my head, probably for decades. The contaminating white noise has slipped off like an albatross from a neck, falling on a deck stagnant upon a still sea. When silence is deep, you hear it. Quiet is a distinct thing, with a voice of its own, a posture that is not tense, a present that is not isolating, a stillness that is not merely the absence of noise. This silence does not dissolve in the presence of chatter. It is not disturbed. It is not soluble. In time, I will recognize this, devoid of emotion, fear, need, the clenching up in preparedness for what may or may not be coming at me, to be peace.

Day 6

Wear Your Battle Scars

I FEEL LIKE A WARRIOR RIDING INTO BATTLE TODAY. I am wounded. I am carrying the pain, not just of this one birth, but of those long past. I have excavated proof of their existence from under my skin if you need it. Ask me what it means to carry lifetimes within a life. Have you ever carried another man's backpack while on a trek over a mountain, even for just a while? You can hand it back when he finds his energy again. Here I am carrying the burdens of my many selves, one after the other, without respite, without even knowing it. Who will I hand the burden of my selves to when I am done?

I have walked such a distance, in so many kinds of weather, that my skin is marked with scars. From stubbed toes to that crick in my neck from three bodies ago, to knife wounds and slashes, healed over with bumpy uneven stitches that run in gashes down my body. Look closely and you will see that all encounters, however negligible, leave evidence on the body. On my forehead, where I bumped into a wall while playing hide-and-seek. On my arm, where I ran into the barbed wire fence while playing chor–police. On my knee, where it grazed the gravel when I fell off my bicycle. There, where my first puppy broke in his first teeth, and there, where there were too many mosquitoes on that holiday. Whether my mind can recall them or not, my skin is scripted with the ink of my past actions, like an unpublished memoir lying in my drawer. These are just the ones I can show you. There are others you cannot witness with me, or whose stories I myself have no words to convey.

I know them by the sharp stabs to the uterus. Quiet embers burning away in my stomach. The grating in my throat. The itch on my tongue. My spine hunching over like Atlas under his rock. I see now that the language of the forgotten is pain. I notice the soles of my feet, the bones in the arches burn as though I have been walking for days down paths I do not know with no rest. I don't know my own quests; I have just come to the realization I have them. It stirs a thirst, but I am in no mood to rise and quench it. Today, I savour my thirst. Even my shins have stopped craving attention, quietened like drama queens hushed in their flailing by a real empress of tragedy. On my clavicle lies a heaviness. In my chest, a weight. On the nape of my neck is the grief of burial grounds.

I travel along the map of my body the pain draws for me, revealing a country I did not know simmered quietly beneath. I connect the dots, on a journey between the gaps, from one pain to the next. On the highways are interludes brought by the shade of tall trees and oases of fresh spring water. There are dips in the ocean, bringing wetness, cleanness, tingling in the sun, or simply nothingness. Absence occurs in nooks and crannies between the hills and valleys, the highs and lows. The non-participation of the left hand in the crimes of the right, the ears that convey without comment, the inner depth of the elbow, the pit of the navel, the back of the knees, silently bringing up the rear, standing back as though what the rest of the body does will not impact them. The numb vagina that simply does not want to speak. Perhaps they have had voices and choices and pains too, but have become accustomed to staying silent, aware they are not seen and will not be heard. We have all sat in a quorum like that. I see them now, and while I revisit them repeatedly, linger at their doors, wait for their response, they are withdrawn. I receive their silence knowing full well they have stories to tell. I am beginning to remember some of them. But they must arrive at their revelations at their own pace. We all do. I tell them I am moving on for now, but I will return periodically to listen again. If I come back repeatedly, they will come to a faith that this time she really wants to know. If not today, then tomorrow, or the day after, or many days after that. Someday surely, they will forgive me for the years of neglect and open up. Come in, they will say, and offer me a drink of water, and I will listen to them weep. I am here now. I am present. I am aware. I am focused. All of them still will not yield to me, but I am the all-consuming occupant of these cells assigned to me, accumulated by my actions, chosen out of all the other matter that wasn't brought home to make me.

I refuse to be unknowing of me any more.

I can no longer say, 'I don't know why I did what I did.' Why I ate that extra bowl of rice. Or reached for the ice cream. Or shouted in anger. Or wept in sorrow. Or trembled in fear. Or left. At least for everything that I have done till now, I know exactly why.

Every time I reach for an object, it creates a sensation in me. The rice brings me a sensation of home, rootedness, where I come from. Of my grandmother and her pillowy shovelfuls of rice. The ice cream makes me feel satiated, the cool brings solace to the inside of my mouth. When I shout, I am erecting that force field again, which protects me from the object of my anger. When I weep, I am longing to rebuild my self-image to what I think it should be. When I fear, I want to control outcomes and am rejecting the unknown. No two emotions or sensations are the same, but each is interlinked.

Little that I do fulfils an external need. Most of my actions serve to assuage these sensations. I don't eat because I need the food, I eat to feel how I felt when I last ate that. This is the source of all cravings. Wanting to feel good, full, fulfilled, satiated, whole, loved, belonging again. Cravings reinforce the positive sensations. Aversions reinforce escape from the bad. Ergo, I don't drink to consume alcohol, I drink to feel how alcohol makes me feel. I don't exercise to practise the action, I do it to feel a sense of control over my body.

All my addictions, obsessions, habits, cultivated practices, predictable reactions fulfil this function. Why do I need the control? Or rather, what do I lack control over that I need to fulfil that sensation? I knock at my doors till I am open. When I am open, the fear, the anger, the need dissipates like an odour that simply needed to be aired out.

I scan myself now from the top of my head to the tip of my little toe. 'Then,' the Teacher says, 'reverse the direction. Go back up the way you came. Look at yourself from up to down, down to up, back to front, front to back, till the alphabet of your existence strings together meaning from every perspective.' I am embarrassed to meet my spine. It has been quietly holding me up through everything I presumed I went through alone, not complaining, not giving way, not seeking credit. Just determined and unwavering in its support. As I travel up and down its length now, I see it is compressed in places, dented in others, tattered, worn, weary, throbbing, yet steady. How little I have known myself. How devoid of compassion I have been towards all that has held me up. How thoughtlessly I have kept adding to my own burdens. The spine has taken the brunt of it.

I am here to make amends now.

The Teacher sings:

Bhogata bhogata bhogate
baṅdhana bandhthe jāyaṅ;

dekhata dekhata dekhate
baṅdhana khulate jāyaṅ

Rolling and rolling in the pleasures of our senses,
we keep tying knots;
observing, observing, observing,
we release ourselves from the knots.

All my body asks of me is that I do nothing that adds to its pain. That I hear its pain. I have offered it an abusive relationship instead. Till today, I have thought that the pain came from things that were done to me. From sitting for long hours, walking, overexertion at work or play. But pain comes to the body from so many more places – from words misspoken, from dreams held in, from simmering anger, from unspoken love, from harbouring great grief. I see now that doing two more sets at the gym were not all that made my shoulders sore. Overeager personal trainers are not the bane of my existence.

I have only learnt this by stepping back, shutting down and watching. That is all I have done for six days now. Watch my body with my mind, using both as instruments to scope the other out, sometimes broadly and sometimes minutely. I am learning that this composite is me – it holds my secrets, tells my tales, reveals me, better than any friend or foe ever can.

I think of a man whom I have been angry at for a long while. Every time I think of him, I notice a corresponding stabbing pain located in the middle of my back. The pain is long, and shaped like 'Oumuamua, the intergalactic interloper scientists spotted in 2017. It is elongated and flat, like an obelisk that runs down a sliver of my back. Every time I think of him, I feel a sharp sensation here. I let him, it, go, and move on to other thoughts, bringing my focus back to other parts of my body, rotating my attention from top to bottom, bottom to top, cyclically. I have discovered a way to peek at the assistant teacher's clock, on a pillar facing him that I have not noticed before. With its help, I know now that each complete meditation cycle takes me around ten minutes to finish. Sometimes, when I am restless, I speed it up and finish it up in five minutes, and open my eyes for the rest of the time. When it is group-sitting that requires aditthana, I am not able to close my eyes for more than three quarters of an hour. I have to move and open them for a peek around that time. When I am lost in my thoughts, sometimes the mind wanders off for the whole session, up to an hour and a half. So it's not like I can't do it. Merely that, just because we have been told to stay firm for this one hour, my rebellious mind won't. This is how my son used to be about brinjal. He loved it when he was little, but the day someone told him it was good for him and he ought to eat it often, he began to reject it. Aditthana is my brinjal. We are all like this in some way. The mind speaks the language of manipulation, demanding it as much as it administers it. I don't play that game any more. So,

I let it stage its mini protest march for one and refuse to apply force. When I return to my back in one of the rounds, I fall short of breath due to my bronchitis and breathe in deeply. That's when I notice the 'Oumuamua moving. That's when it strikes me. It is not located in my back. It is the shape of my right lung that I am feeling the pain in. It is so acutely outlined with pain because of the bronchitis. It carries so much pain that it is distinct in shape and form. Worse, every time I think of the man I do not like, I am adding to the pain it carries. I am literally choking myself on my anger.

The realization comes like an X-ray to a smoker, outlining the residue in his lungs. This is what I have done to myself. Nobody suffers from my anger but me. Nobody has caused me to walk around with this particular pain but me. There is that Zen saying, holding on to anger is like a holding a burning ember – the only person affected is you. Memes are lovely until you actually see what they mean. Then, they're terrifying. The only person I am hurting, physically, literally, in the now, by my anger, is me. I say this over and over again to myself, tossing its permutations about in my head till it really sinks in. It has meant years of unnecessary inhalers, coughing, pain in the chest, medication, discomfort – for what? Because someone said something to me twenty years ago? What a waste of a life, of mind space, of sentiment. The response of rage in my mind towards this person who elicits it evaporates in an instant. I drop the thought of him like it has singed my palm. Never again, I vow, will I allow myself to waste my emotion of anger towards another. Sometimes I will have to show it, to make a point, to scold, to set right. But never will I allow myself to feel it. It's something my father used to say when I first became a mother: 'Never feel anger when you scold a child; only show it.' Today I truly understand what it means.

Today is not an eventful day, but it is not a negligible one either. It is smooth, like a mellow tune playing in the background. It is harmonized and jarring in all the right places.

It is heavily overcast in the afternoon, and we run to gather our drying clothes from the porch. The wind has blown the chairs over and banged the windows shut. Rain constantly quivers on the lip of the wind, but it quickly regains its composure.

On my way back to the hall, I see Jessica seated on the second step of the walkway, her head between her knees, sobbing uncontrollably. At least I think she is crying. Her shawl is drawn over her back and head, so I can't tell for sure. I wonder what to do. I consider retreating and giving her her privacy. But she shakes like a tendril from a creeper, caught in the wind and in need of anchor. Her ears have turned bright red. I consider my energy. We are not supposed to touch each other because we transfer energy, positive and negative, between us. I think about each of us. I don't know too much about the others and their pains, but I know we all have them.

I contemplate my own. It will take lifetimes for me to cleanse them. I didn't think I was going to be the Buddha by the end of this course anyway. Maybe I can be the Buddha next time. This time, all I can be is human. Maybe that is all that some of us lesser buddhas will ever be – compassionate. I sit down next to her and put my arms around her. She collapses onto my shoulder, weeping, and we sit there, saying nothing for a few minutes, until she has stopped trembling. I feel a little guilt for allowing myself to be involved in this but think to myself: It's okay, I'll just do the course again. There is something inevitable about the collapse of our boundaries, an acknowledgement that even as we strive as individuals, our collective inability to simply walk past the utter grief of another keeps us human. The spiritual progress of each of the sangha's members becomes as vital as our own. As the outpouring of emotion fades to a trickle, we separate. I go back into the meditation hall and she continues to sit where she was. We will never mention it again.

When I sit down now, I do not sit alone. I gather my pains and joys to my body and take them along. We are one, an entourage of sensation, an internal sorority much like our little external one, making our way together. Wherever I go, all the newly awakened sensations that I have felt must come with me. Some will break journey along the line. Some will disappear. Some will stay the course. They will live in me, but I will not live in them. I house them, for how they have served me. I cannot reject them for I have summoned them. I must acknowledge them and love them too.

The chants of Day 6 are from the Paṭiccasamuppāda, the key insight from the night Gautama, the Buddha attained his liberation. It is referred to as the Chain of Conditioned Arising.

Avijjā-paccayā saṅkhārā;
saṅkhāra-paccaya viññāṇaṃ;
viññāṇa-paccayā nāma-rupaṃ;
nāma-rupa-paccayā salāyatanaṃ;
salāyatana-paccayā phasso;
phassa-paccayā vedanā;
vedana-paccaya taṇha;
taṇha-paccaya upādanaṃ;
upādana paccayā bhavo;
bhava-paccayā jāti;
jāti-paccaya jara-maraṇaṃ
soka-parideva
dukkha-domanassupāyasā
sambhavanti
evamettassa kevalasa dukkhakhandassa
samudayo hoti'ti

With the base of ignorance, reaction arises.
With the base of reaction, consciousness arises.
With the base of consciousness, mind and body arise.

With the base of mind and body, the six senses arise.
With the base of the six senses, contact arises.
With the base of contact, sensation arises.
With the base of sensation, craving and aversion arise.
With the base of craving and aversion, attachment arises.
With the base of attachment, becoming arises.
With the base of becoming, birth arises.
With the base of birth, ageing and death arise, together with sorrow, lamentation, physical and mental sufferings and tribulations; thus arises the entire mass of suffering.

The verse runs in reverse too. As each is removed, the corresponding layer of bondage is peeled back. To witness this sequence as it unfolds is vipassana. To know the pattern is to see it play out in one's self.

The Teacher warns you not to be entrapped in the interludes or be caught up in denial of the pain. Both must be treated with equanimity. It is good that both are occurring together in my body right now, because I can equate them simultaneously. This pain, this joy, both passing, dissipate over the next five rounds of meditation, only to reappear in another. In a way, it's not really equanimous, I tell the Teacher, in my head. I can

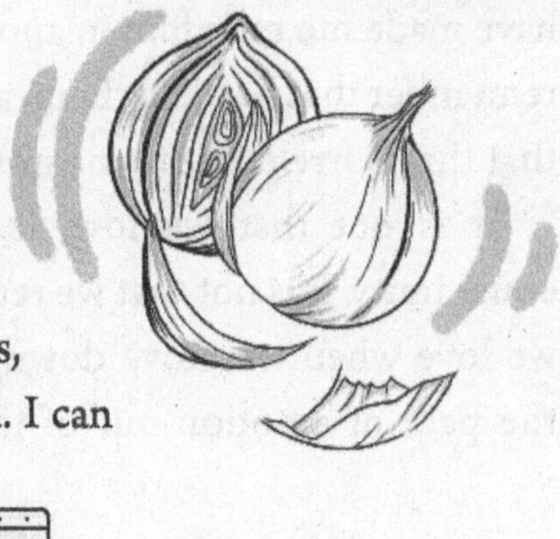

love my pain, but I can never hate my joys. 'It's not love; it's longing,' he warns me. 'It's craving. You can't crave pain – that would make you a masochist. You are better off cultivating indifference.' I remember what a former lover once told me when we broke up: 'Hate me if you must, but your indifference will be worse than death, because it will mean that I have ceased to matter.' Well, darling, I whisper to my pain now, you've ceased to matter.

I think of the lover without a sense of loss. It is not that I think of him without a sense of joy. They are two different things. It is the difference between a memory, and a memory that brings you pain. It is the difference between not caring as an act of anger, and not caring because one views it as a leaf in a river that was headed downstream to the sea anyway. I remember you, but not with pain. You do not drive me, either away or closer. You are. I am. We were. That is all it is. I will remember this teaching on the way down the hillside when the Wizzride taxi driver will play old Hindi songs for several hours. Songs that would have made me miss him in another life. But this time, I will remember that he liked them, and then I will remind myself that that is irrelevant to me now.

It is not that we love less when we begin to seek equanimity. It is not that we remain unmoved by the people we love when we move down this path. It is that we take the pain of emotion out of the interaction. When I love you with emotion, I also turn away from you with emotion. Now, I just accept you, whatever you may be. Perhaps we love more this way because we do not tie in our love with expectation. Those we love can never disappoint us because we wanted nothing to begin with. Those we hate cannot infuriate us because we did not seek their love and it becomes so easy to reject their hate. Our actions towards them come from a space of equanimity. I am not capable of anger at you any more because, and don't take this the wrong way, I don't need you. Your reactions don't excite me any more than mine do. It is easy to misunderstand this as a living death. But that is only so when this turning away comes from the negative, when one is fed up, when one harbours resentment. You will always have my compassion. You have merely lost the power to evoke a corresponding sensation in me. You could send me purple orchids or a box of abuses, and both will seem the same.

The more pain manifests, the more it acts out. There is only one release, and that is compassion – for myself, for everything I have acted and reacted for, for every vedana, or sensation, I am carrying. I do not wish them gone; I do not wish them to stay. Like a polite host, I offer them shelter. They are welcome to stay as long as they wish to. When they are done, they will make their way to their destinations.

I just know that now it is impossible for me to walk alone any more. So many walls have broken down, within and without, that the sangha is forming. On my travels, I will stop at Sewagram, Wardha, to chat with the school principal of the Nai Taalim school. She will ask me if meditation means isolating oneself, losing a sense of responsibility towards one's fellowman. 'If a mob is running amuck, would you close your eyes and think that violence is them, not me, and turn away?' she will ask. In my experience, the more inward you go, the more the outward dissolves. If you truly see, then you see that there is no other, as Ramana Maharshi said. You see a mob reacting from a place of pain, acting as a collective when they are individuals, acting as individuals when they are all interconnected. You can only send them compassion and the hope that they come to the realization too. They harm no other but themselves. The Teacher will explain in tonight's discourse that the correct practice of vipassana will make one more active, not inactive. This is because so far you have lived only in terms of reactions, but once you have discovered how and why you react, you are able to now take actions more deliberately, precisely and knowingly. The more you watch yourself, the more you realize the ways in which you are constantly reacting. With every reaction, another kalapa arises and settles within you. Every reaction, either present or past, is settling inside you. It settles like a fine layer of dust in a room that hasn't been opened in years. We clean our rooms out every day, especially here in India. I think of that line in Upamanyu Chatterjee's *English, August* about the mark the lady who wipes the floor leaves on all Indian walls, where her washcloth touches the whitewash. We don't clear out our minds every day, and the more the layers of dust piles up, the more we react to its stockpile, the more marks we generate. I have to now release the dust and not react in a way that leaves marks on the wall. It's a delicate dance.

There are obstacles, of course. The Teacher lists five. I could list ten more. He doesn't have the disadvantage of having his mind meander. When he speaks now, he assumes we're all focused on the meditation. I go along with the assumption. Don't want to upset the teachers. But sometimes I'm thinking about my son and sometimes I am wondering if there is any way to order pizza for dinner, meet the delivery guy at the gate and eat it in the forest in the dark among the leeches before I return to my room. Good thing they took my phone away. Yes, the Teacher doesn't list this among one of the obstacles, so I will not go to the assistant teacher today and say, 'Um...but...' They think me better than that, so I will try to be.

The first obstacle the Teacher describes is craving and the second is its companion, aversion. He believes, kind soul, that my craving stops at wanting pleasant subtle sensations. 'Even craving subtle sensations and cultivating an aversion to the painful ones sends one in the opposite direction,' he warns. How far at the back of the line am I, huh? I bring my mind back to doing its rounds, but it is stubborn, especially this late in the evening. It wants to wander.

As if on cue, the Teacher pronounces laziness and drowsiness as the third enemy of the mind. I am sheepish. Why do we fall asleep during meditation even after a whole night of sound sleep? It is the impurities in the mind that cause its heaviness. This also links back to the alertness you feel, not inactiveness, as a meditator. You do more.

The fourth enemy is restlessness, though the Teacher calls it agitation. I also call it writer's block. I know it well. I run around, decide I have to clean out the fridge this very instant, Marie Kondo my neglected-for-years cupboard, and pay a visit to the doctor to take a random blood test to ensure I don't have diabetes or cancer for no reason whatsoever. Anything but write ... um ... meditate. I know such days well.

'The final enemy is doubt,' the Teacher pronounces. I think back to Day 5. Doubt is also mentally crippling. It paralyses you, like suspicion in a marriage. When I was deciding to get divorced, my father had said that my husband and I were like an imaginary dog chasing an imaginary cat. That is what doubt is like. Once it grips you, there is very little you can do except have one of the imaginary creatures catch the other and eat it for lunch. Or, you know, just go watch a *Lost* marathon or something, until they resolve their chase themselves. Take your mind off it. I once wanted to buy a house and was dead set on it until someone in my family asked an astrologer if the house would be good for me. He said there was a very pissed off devi in the house who would trouble anyone who took charge of the place without making suitable arrangements for her propitiation. Never mind that the owner had been living there quite comfortably for many years and had prospered. No matter how hard I tried to get over it, I simply couldn't. What if, yeah? What if? My son, the atheist, of course, held his sides and ROFLMAO-ed at me. Here I was, letting go of a house I absolutely loved, at a price that worked for me, because of the seed of doubt someone had sowed in my mind. It's just so easy to come into doubt – so immensely hard to shake it off. We entertain doubts because we think we are resolving our own ambiguity, but how long do you let that seed grow? I think of Peter and Jesus. In the Book of Luke, after a whole night of toiling, Jesus fills Peter's nets with fish and tells him, 'Be not afraid. From now you have to catch men.' So doesn't doubt also lead you to answers? Doesn't doubt, even self-doubt, keep us humble and self-aware? My best friend is a counsellor at a church back home, and I make a mental note to ask her what purpose Peter's doubt served. Doubt is what leads you to answers, I suspect. But then, one doesn't want to be a doubting Thomas either, feeling the wounds in order to believe. We live in an age now where belief, faith are all becoming very difficult to profess because people keep letting us down. Wouldn't it be folly now to say we believe in someone, say a leader or a star, sometimes even a teacher or a mentor? I don't even believe news reports, and I work in the media. I think of the women vowing they have faith in the character of some man they believe to be good, but who is accused of harassment by someone else. It sounds so self-defeating to make these statements of faith, because the truth is, we don't really ever know. We've all met those silver-tongued foxes who profess undying love and integrity until their wives turn up with rolling pins in their hands! The gentlemen rakes. Yikes! It is better today to not believe blindly. It is actually better to doubt. Didn't the Teacher also say, 'Don't take my word for it, don't take the Buddha's word for it – experiencing the truth for yourself is the highest form of truth.' So what is the end of doubt? My guess is it would be doubt for doubt's sake. Like that game children play, 'But, mama, why?' – repeating the same question until it takes you down a rabbit hole. I suspect a small dose of faith is also necessary. But vipassana doesn't speak about faith. There is no faith; there is only do–experience–feel.

This to me is another paradox, but I have faith that it is not that the answers are not there, but that I am not experienced and advanced enough to know them. So I set aside my doubts for now and tell myself I am getting ahead of myself. I must focus on what level of proficiency I can achieve here. Even I can see that allowing this chain of doubt to keep going endlessly obstructs my ability to focus on the practice. It comes from my impatience to know, to have all the answers, have them all now, when I want them. There is so much ego in that too. The answers come when you've done the work, and that's not faith, that's experience. My smaller answers have come. The big ones will too. I vow tonight to extricate myself from doubt's glutenous grip and keep walking.

My roomie and I catch each other's eye at the light switch and smile in passing, quickly looking away. What once seemed an intrusion now isn't.

Day 7

Go Over the Mountain

ARVIND KEJRIWAL IN A MUFFLER AND AN AAM AADMI cap coughing away at a podium pops up in my morning meditation today. I remember him well, a sweaty boxer on an *India Today* cover, he was constantly doing battle. He would call press conferences and thrust his fists into the air propagating conspiracy like Mel Gibson in an aluminium hat. I haven't seen him do that in quite a while. I was among those who sneered that at crucial times during his campaign or his new-found chief ministership of Delhi, the tiny self-righteous man seemed to take off to what seemed to be some sort of a wellness retreat for days together. How irresponsible, I had thought then. I wonder where he's gone now. Though I have no way of knowing, I'm pretty sure his problems haven't ceased. His antagonists haven't disappeared. And governmental headbutting is a routine part of getting work done. I learnt later that he had headed to a vipassana course. Perhaps he has simply learnt not to react to his antagonists and get on with his work. Delhi is still standing, after all. It will, however, burn later, and those who believed in him will blame him for inaction. I will wonder then if he is being inactive or non-reactive. Perhaps he did what was needed and not what was visible. I will hope he responded to what was needed in that moment, and base it on knowing that this form of rigorous meditation puts a pause to our actions.

I put political thoughts out of my mind for now and focus on the verses for the day.

Main main main hī janama kā
jarā mṛutyū kā mūla
aham bhāva miṭe binā
miṭe na bhava bhaya śula

Self-centredness, this is the cause of birth,
decay and death,
unless the ego is removed,
the torment and fear of existence will not stop.

Me, me, me, me, me. Our lives revolve around ourselves; our problems appear huge because they impact us, and our meditations are quite simply about making our lives easier, more meaningful, whatever. Considering all of Eastern philosophy is about the self, it's a bit rich to ask us not to focus on ourselves so much. This is a paradox of our culture I have not been able to resolve for myself. How does focusing on my self help me reduce my focus on myself, which, apparently, is the only path to breaking this circle of self-absorption? Yeah, solve that one and I can see why they say you will have seen the light.

I have achieved some modicum of focus now, by the seventh day. I am able to scan myself for at least an hour. I have discovered the clock on the pillar that the assistant teacher looks at to stop and start sessions, and, if I discreetly lean forward, I find I am able to more precisely time my meditations. One complete scan is up and down and then from the toes back up again, two to one set, like my grandfather who did his Surya Namaskar sets on the terrace used to count them. Each set takes me five minutes now. My speed has increased and my focus is better. It is precise to the swagger of the arm of the clock; even if I think I have had a super session and open my eyes, it stays precisely at five minutes a round. This is great! I now have an internal clock

and I just have to count my rounds to know what time it is! Don't even have to open my eyes! Alas, this just brings up a whole host of other distractions. Like how many rounds to lunch or tea or a pee break. Labelling my sensations (this painful thing settling in my lungs is anger or sadness; that one is joy) and timing my meditations are both a really bad idea, I quickly see. Not good. I have also fallen into the trap of completing my rounds and checking with the clock to see if my estimated time is correct. It becomes a meaningless game my mind has started to play. Even when you think you are focusing, you are not. I remember the Teacher's warnings of the kinds of obstacles from Day 6. They are immensely useful. When you know what to look for, you are able to neatly skip over the outstretched leg it extends to trip you up. I look back to raise an eyebrow at the neat entrapment I almost fell for. Ha! You don't get to suck me in this time, I think as I go back to my scans. Good god! I'm talking to myself, I sound positively insane. But then, I remember what the Teacher said on Day 1: 'If we listen to our minds long enough, we realize how devoid of logic and rationale we really sound.' I shut it down like I do the neighbour aunty who thinks writing is not really a full-time job and wants to interrupt my work to discuss the more important fact of what Desai uncle on third floor is doing in his bid for society secretary.

I have come to rely on the verses of the chants now. They become the peg that holds my attention while I catapult myself back to a state of concentration. Don't shlokas and other chants, forms also perform the same role, I wonder. Perhaps the problem is we get too attached to them, and find comfort in the way they make us feel. We cultivate a reliance on the rhythm, sound, the images they evoke. The recollection of my grandmother singing the Vishnu Sahasranama is inevitable if I listen to the chant, and meditation is then not devoid of association. Even here, even with a Teacher who warns us of these attachments, I realize there is a very real danger of latching on to him; like baby ducks, we are clinging to his form, his voice, his words. These all become entrapments.

Jab tak mann meṅrāag hai
jab tak mann meṅdvesa;
tab tak duhkha hi duhkha hai
miten na mann ke kleśa

As long as there is craving in the mind,
as long as in the mind is aversion,
there will be suffering, only suffering –
the mind cannot be purged of affliction.

I am not feeling too much anger today at anyone, so I tend to take this like a Bohri passing the salt over the thaal, with a pinch of ritualistic sanguinity. I feel an imaginary smack at the back of my head. Maybe I shouldn't be so arrogant as to think I have resolved my resentment issues. It will take years to think of people who have hurt me and really release the feelings of anger I have towards them; I am aware of this. When my grandmother died, she was angry at a whole lot of people and scolded them as she was dying. I felt bad for her, and sorry for those whom she left behind, fearful of her anger. She was a loving, kind woman all her life, always correct, always mindful of her duties and responsibilities, and a true matriarch whom everyone respected. She was the kind of straight-talking woman whom extended family or friends had come to rely on. Then to die with so much pent-up anger... it has left me wishing she had been able to resolve it for herself sooner. The Teacher mentions Jesus in one discourse. The sign of a truly enlightened man is one who is able to speak with compassion and forgiveness at the time of death. The preoccupation with our wrongs is something I've seen in many older people over the years. As we get closer to death, when our children have left home, when our day jobs cease to consume our every waking hour, and when we have more help and less to do around the house, the voids in our lives expand. We are filled then with memories of things we wish we had done and said. Resentment towards the people who should have and could have made our lives easier crops up. When we become overwhelmed with these feelings, it is often a surprise to both the person feeling it and the person at the receiving end of it. These are often repressed issues that have not been spoken of for decades. As older people begin to ramble, I switch off, thinking, *Oh, here they go again*. When I do listen, I realize these are lifelong regrets that are wasting them away from the inside out – 'the job I should have taken', 'the salary I could have earned', 'the journeys I never undertook', 'the partner I didn't choose', 'the property I didn't fight for', 'the opportunities that should have been mine', 'the relationships I didn't repair'. A lot of these are also free to come up at this late stage of life because these people are no longer bound by their old fears. The proximity to death makes them somehow fearless now, and that allows them to know how they really feel about things. Until now they said the correct thing, or the expected thing, wary of the consequences. Assuming none of us really know when we are going to die, we live now, in this moment, with unresolved resentment simmering away somewhere within us. I don't want to wait for death – rather, given the rate at which everyone around is getting cancer, and my highly toxic lifestyle, I will be lucky if I get another ten years, so I better start resolving things now. Sitting here and smugly telling myself that I don't feel anger is not going to help me in the least.

I decide I need a break and take a stroll by the outdoor pantry. The pile of ladies' fingers in the corner has diminished, so I am guessing that's for lunch today. I spot the long brinjals still there and hope maybe we will get that tomorrow. I was trying not to overeat, but there was some deep-fried homemade alo balep, a Tibetan bread with potato curry, for breakfast today, and I couldn't resist taking two. Flaky, circular, semi-sweet diskettes dipped in spicy gravy with broken potatoes – super yum! I wish I could talk just to be able to take down recipes. It is a gloomy day today and the hot food is invigorating. Our silences have become more comfortable now. Diana and Mrs Pradhan seem to be in some sort of silent communion every day, with eyes only for each other. We are each better adjusted to being left alone with our thoughts. I remember that tweet by Dave Vescio that became a meme floating about the Internet in various permutations now: 'I saw a guy at Starbucks today. No iPhone. No tablet. No laptop. He just sat there. Drinking coffee. Like a psychopath.' We're all that guy now.

In the afternoon session, Diana bursts into a loud sob. We have become accustomed to each other's predilections and quirks by now, but we are still disturbed when another is upset. We may be working on our own, but the breakdown of one affects the whole sangha. She runs outside and breaks into a full-scale wail just as she reaches the porch of the meditation hall. She thinks she is alone now and releases her pent-up emotions, but we can hear her clearly. She cannot go back to the house because it is raining cats and dogs, and even above the pelting of the rain on the roof, we hear her wring her heart out. I want to go out to her, like she has for so many of us these past few days. That is just who Diana is, or seems to me at any rate. I also know now that she must work this out on her own. Releasing one's grief is a deeply personal and intense experience, and I have learnt the lessons of not intervening, not obstructing and, most importantly, not reacting. I feel a tinge of guilt for holding Jessica yesterday. I should have left her alone too. But she seemed a little girl lost, and my mothering instinct kicked in. I realize I held her more for myself than for her. We each react for ourselves. We just tell ourselves we do it for others. So, as much as it pains me, I sit there in the hall listening to her cry. My thoughts eventually wander, and I go back to my meditation as her sobs cease. The rain has abated, and when I leave the hall for a pee break a good half hour later, I find her still lying on the floor of the porch, her back flat against its cold stone, silently crying. I go back in and whisper to Dechen. Perhaps she could tell her to go to her room and rest, or comfort her? Dechen suggests we let her be. 'It's raining, and the floor is cold,' I protest. She nods and leaves the hall to talk to her.

Today, I am deeply aware I lack equanimity. Reacting, and then following that thread of thought and action that it loosens from the soil, is instinct to me. I see the world too much. I want to know and do too much. When the assistant teacher calls us, he asks if we feel calm. I truthfully tell him I lack that stillness. 'It will take time,' he says. 'Even for those of us who have been doing this for forty years, it takes time to get there.' I feel strangely comforted that I am not struggling alone, though I do think I am probably the weakest student in class. My mind is a roller coaster, enough to fill a book, eh? I envy those who have fewer, better-catalogued thoughts.

The verses of Day 7 are from the Bhojjhaṅgaparitta, and are verses of protection from the Bhojjhaṅga-samyutta of the Samyutta-nikāya. The Buddha had two disciples, Moggallana and Kassapa, who received help in their illness from chanting these verses that he taught them.

Bhojjhaṅgo satisaṅkhato
dhammānam vicayo tathā
viriyam piti passaddhi
bhojjhaṅgā ca tathā pare
samādhupekkhā bhojjhaṅgā
sattate sabbadassinā;
muninā sammadakkhātā
bhāvitā bahulīkatā.

The factors of enlightenment, namely, awareness,
analytical investigation of dhamma,
effort, bliss and tranquillity,
are factors of enlightenment, and the others,
concentration and equanimity,
these seven were well-taught,
practised and cultivated
by the all-seeing sage.

How do you know that you are getting enlightened? Unlike other techniques that tell you to wait for the afterlife, in vipassana, the results are immediate. If it is working, you will know. You will acquire these qualities or traces of them in the immediate moment. Nothing about this technique is ambiguous. It is a nursery workbook that comes with scented stickers and a big smiley next to the tick mark when you've done well.

Just as there are enemies and obstacles to meditation, so too there are friends. The first is faith. Ha, I think, I was right. Inside, I think I am relieved. I have always been enamoured by the idea of a leap of faith, which is why I love the Fool in tarot cards so much. If Fool I must be, that is fine. We must not lose our instinct to trust each other. What is love, after all, without giving someone the power to hurt you, all the while trusting that they won't? We each carry the intrinsic hope that there is that good instinct in another that would suggest they uphold your faith in them. And the same in me for others. Without it, we are all just walking disappointments.

It comes with a caveat though. Blind faith is an enemy, but with discrimination, it can be used to find inspiration in people we would like to emulate. It shows us where we want to go. 'Put your faith,' says the Teacher, 'not in persons, but in the qualities of the person. Instead of the Buddha as a wise man, put the faith in his particular qualities that you want to acquire. Then, you will neither be disappointed, nor will your faith be blind.' Faith in Buddha, in dhamma, in sangha comes this way. Qualities that set to inspire you, that have you emulate them, that you see the results of, that spread to others, non-sectarian, non-divisive, universal, experiential. Find the qualities that something contains, and distinguish them from the overall, generic version. Then we will be able to say to idols with feet of clay: 'I respected you because you had integrity, but you don't now, so you no longer hold my faith.' We are then not broken by people who disappoint us; we are able to take the good from them and leave them to their follies. So also, effort, awareness, concentration, wisdom. I like the line where the Teacher says, 'You cannot be aware of the past, you can only remember it. You don't know the future, so awareness can only ever be of the absolute present moment.' I find this revelatory, as though I had unwrapped a toffee and found a nugget of gold inside, the idea that there is not even awareness of the past, only memory, because when something has gone, it is instantaneous in its passing. And here we all are, still shedding tears and harbouring resentment for things that happened so very long ago. Breakfast is in the past now. How does it matter what we had, or what happened at it? It's over. Gone. Nothing about it can be transformed or set right or improved. We couldn't possibly have upma instead. Then, what of an argument a decade ago? Nothing that has happened can unhappen. No outcomes resulting from it can be changed. We can only be aware of the now, and not react to anything that happens now or that derives from what happened then. The futility of it becomes so stark that the present becomes an overwhelming, all-consuming one. All that exists is now. In the now, my son is not here, nor my dog, my home, my investments, my office, my colleagues, my deadlines, my family, my parents, my exes, my future, not even my dreams and hopes for tomorrow, my pending lists of to-dos and must-reads. Nothing exists but the now, a pulsing, throbbing, living thing in this instant. Leg ache and pouring rain and how many rounds I fluidly achieve. Nothing else matters.

I have been feeling an urge to jot this all down, the free-flowing discovery of my mind as the meditation progresses, but have been wondering if that would be allowed. In the middle of his speech the Teacher suddenly says, 'If you have been feeling the urge to write, go ahead. That is the nature of dhamma – you want to share it, you want others to benefit from it; that is how you know it is working.' I begin to recapitulate the past seven days in my mind in bullet form, making mental notes for later. It is uncanny how he manages to respond to most of the thoughts and questions that come up in your mind during the day, even the most trivial of them. I admit it, I have begun to bow to the TV now after every session. I utter 'Sadhu Sadhu Sadhu' wholeheartedly. I contemplate converting to Buddhism. I know I could do this meditation for the rest of my life. I have visions of undertaking the sixty-day course in a solitary cell under the golden pagoda, and my son coming to visit me on his holidays. I wonder what to do with my dog – I don't want to abandon him. Maybe the sangha can adopt him and he can become a monastery dog. He will be fed and he will be around me. I wonder if they will give him meat. Am I a Buddhist now? I like the Buddha. He was no-nonsense. He was tired of the highfalutin philosophers and was like, Yeah, yeah, get to the point. Where is the ladder to a higher realm? And when they couldn't and wouldn't explain it to him, he found it himself. And he made it accessible. In the initial days, I had wondered if they shouldn't have more stringent sign-up mechanisms, but now I realize that those who can't stay the course won't anyway. That's not for me or them or anyone else to decide. The path will decide along

with the aspirant. What is that Irish saying? May the path rise up to greet you on your way. Dhamma is like that. These choices are not ours to make for ourselves, let alone for others. I think about the more closed-circuit philosophies of the world, the inner circles of learning. Their language elevated, their practices rigorous, secretive and probably not for everyone. If it works and is functional, it must be simple and direct. This must be a quality of learning that is efficient. If it fails to communicate with a student and simplify the complex, then it needs an explainer, another guide, and then we are creating a system that is rigged with obstacles. There is a fearlessness about this discovery, which is why it seeks to communicate itself. At the end of each session, the Teacher chants a blessing that bids all beings be happy, but he also chants that may all beings benefit from his spiritual progress. He has called the path a declassified map. Elsewhere, we act like even outlining the road is giving away too much, as though the discovery of the self is to be protected from overcrowding. Like too many spiritually aware people might tilt the balance of the world to the detriment of evil or something. Don't want that happening, huh? How is it sufficient if just I know how to make myself a better person? The only benefit conceivable is that I will not have anyone to uplift and make myself feel superior to. This is again ego. It becomes a craving, for recognition and exaltation, to a display and exercise of learning, a trap that drove even the wise and scholarly Ravana to his misdeeds. In reality, even if you drew everyone that map, they are the ones who still have to find the urge to make the journey and the strength to walk. None of this self-reflection is easy, or, in truth, even necessary, until you feel an inexplicable urge to submerge yourself in it.

We live our lives etherized. You could zone out in front of the nothing-to-bow-about TV and order takeout every night, instead of contemplating your life. Most of us, moi included, do this. It is just easier. Why on earth should I sit and feel my pain? I have enough of it. Give me something that distracts me from my pain, no? Common sense. Except you can do that for only so long, until the urge to get up and change things hits. You get fed up of the bad Chinese or pizza. So you rearrange the furniture, write that manuscript no one will publish, send the kid to college, walk the dog, clean the cupboard, rearrange your stamp collection, and then what? If I could just stop this endless chatter in my head. If I could just stop binge-eating when I don't even like what I'm eating. If I could just stop obsessing over the past, which will never come back. If I could just do something. Then, then, you want a path to walk down and you should have the freedom to explore it. There is no such thing as Buddhism, the Teacher explains, because the Buddha didn't believe in organized religion. He revealed vipassana precisely as a way to cut through the knots of organized religion and inherited knowledge. There is no question of conversion because vipassana is the path to your own mind and body. There is nothing to convert to. You are. It is. And if it is working, and you do get where you want to go, you will realize that the rest is irrelevant anyway. The Buddha as a god and the Buddha as an interior decoration fad are both creations of our need to idolize in different ways. Idolize the qualities, never the man – he wouldn't have been moved by your praise or blame anyway. I instantly think of people – family, friends – whom this system will invigorate. I wish for my son to be able to come here and meditate someday. It took me over ten years from first wanting to till actually arriving here, so I guess everyone must come to their own self-discovery, whatever their path may be, at their own pace. My son is an atheist, a rationalist, and is scornful of all religion, so I know it will take him time to even want to sit and meditate, but I also know that he has a brilliant, sharp, focused mind, and he will see so much more clearly when he does this. I wish for my mother, entangled in her regrets, that she is able to release herself from her sorrows in this way. Though she has come to vipassana before, she has not continued the practice. I hope she is able to get back to it, though now she is too old to sit for such long periods, with a bad knee, so I don't know if it will be possible. Happily, I understand today that I wish this inward drawing for those who have harmed me too. I would not have been able to wish this for them ten days earlier.

There are still twinges of anger when I consider them, but they are laced with sorrow now, that such confrontations happened, that I have thought ill of you, you of me. That we have tackled each other and tumbled down the hill, both of us sustaining injuries in the process. I wish relief from shared hurt, a loosening of the ties that cause us to be inextricably linked in a cycle of action and reaction. That elusive equanimity, the sense that nothing matters, settles briefly in my mind, before it dissipates like buddhi ka baal, candyfloss, in my mouth. Just a momentary taste is enough to let you know you want to feel that equilibrium forever.

By night, the quiver in the sky's lip has blown into a full-scale thunderstorm, sent across the valley by the mountains. The little house shudders and creaks, and I am suddenly grateful it is a back-to-front house. Lightning flashes across the sky and illuminates the valley at intervals. With every roll of thunder, the house rattles like a twig in the mouth of a dog. It rains like the collective heart of the universe is broken. We all lie there, awake in the dark, trying not to react to its pain.

Day 8

Kanchenjunga Rising

THE LIGHT HAS JUST BROKEN ON THE HORIZON AND cuts through the biting cold. For the first time, I have to shuffle my frozen feet along and stuff my numb fingers into my pockets. I head for my pee break and grab a pair of gloves I had stuffed into my suitcase just in case, but haven't had to use so far. The air is crisp, like something is sucking the moisture out of it, a pause that I like to call a snow vacuum whenever I encounter it. It's like sticking your head in a frost-free freezer and feeling the dry air billowing around you. My sister used to do that when she was a kid, coming back home from school on a hot afternoon. The light today is different, clearer, tighter, and, as I approach the hall, I am struck by the urge to look up to know why – and I gasp. The sky is spotless for the first time, an eggshell blue tinged with the gold flecks of the stretching sun. There she is, a haughty manifestation of raw power, billowing soft flakes on sheer rock face, as though she were rocking a baby in a snow blanket between her two precipices. The Kanchenjunga, at 8,586 metres, the third-highest mountain in the world, just staring down at me from across the valley as though she knew all along that I existed just

there, that we all did. She is as fierce as she is awesome. She is so clear, glistening as the light bounces off each of her edges; she seems as though she were outlined and planted there anew, a fresh painting of the storm. She imprints on my mind like a mother duck to a duckling. All through the day, as I shut my eyes, she is what rises in my mind's eye, and with her, the feeling of exaltation, height, the need to rise to the pristine. I cannot even contemplate being an atheist when I see such beauty, because there is no ordinary power that can possibly conceive of it. It is beyond our minds, or at least our conscious ones. I stand there in awe until the morning gong sounds for breakfast. This is my morning meditation. I have no thoughts, at least none I can remember now anyway, except overwhelming awe. The sangha comes tumbling out of the hall doors, rubbing their hands together for warmth. I gesture for them to come quickly, as though the elusive mountain would disappear if they didn't take two steps at a time. I have no recollection of the not-communicating rule, and I wave my hands at them to come quick. 'Kanchenjunga! Kanchenjunga!' we are all repeating over and over to ourselves and each other, as though simply saying her name out loud in some way sanctifies us. Gasps go around the group, from everyone, except the women from Sikkim who probably see her every day. For the rest of us, for me, we are bathing in her clarity, sharing this exultation like choristers around the Rockefeller Centre Christmas tree.

Aptly, the verse for the day is from the Mittānisaṃsa, a poem from the Muga Pakkha Jataka. It tells the story of the bodhisattva born as a prince, Temiya, in Varanasi. He pretends to be deaf and mute all his life to escape performing the ills that his role in power would require him to. He is considered so useless that a woodsman is despatched with him to the woods to execute him. He reveals himself, and his ruse is understood. The king and his court become his followers. Inasmuch a lesson in renunciation, it is a lesson in friendship too.

Aggi yathā pajjalati
devatāva virocati;
siriyā ajahito hoti
yo mittānaṃ na dūbbati

Like fire he shines forth,
like a celestial being he is radiant;
never abandoned by fortune
is he who does not betray his friends.

It leads me to think of the storm last night in all its fury. The raining down, the exorcism of pent-up, crystallized anger also has its purpose. Its purpose is clarity. All our meltdowns haven't been for nothing. Without it, even a view like the one I saw this morning, the greatest view in the world, is obscured. To have these breakthroughs in each other's company is also a reminder that none of us is in this journey of self-discovery alone, although, in the depths of unravelling our despair, it seems like it.

Today, breakfast is steamed Sikkimese bun rolls with chickpea curry. I gobble it down and grab a chair to put in the pathway so that I can gaze upon the mountain some more. It is, in any case, way too cold for a bath. It takes me till mid-afternoon to tear my mind away from Kanchenjunga.

I see now why views are distracting for meditators. Yet, this particular infraction imbues me with calm. Perhaps it is the craving for the pleasant sensation that the Teacher warned us about, the wanting to feel elevated and energized at the subtle level, which is also a trap. 'Don't play the game of sensations,' he warns multiple times in his instructions. 'You'll get sucked into wanting to feel good, not wanting to feel bad. That takes you away from the path.' How bad can it be to want to feel good, eh?

When you get stuck on the sensation, the wanting to feel good, you can't see anything beyond it. Most addictions originate here, he explains. Those of us who repeatedly pray at the altar of food or drugs or alcohol – we are drawn to how it makes us feel, not the item we ingest. Every time I eat, I eat because of the sensation it creates in me. Then when the sensation, temporary, anicya as any, passes, I want to create it again. Cue the addiction. On a larger scale, this is damaging. Our diabetes, our vices, our sugar intake, our

intoxications arise from here. Not being able to recognize this is also why we repeatedly succumb. Now I understand why I cannot stick to diets though I know which ones my body responds well to. Why I don't stick to exercise routines. If I have not eaten for hunger, then all I am doing is chasing the sensation and must repeat the cycle to feel that way again. It all comes down to just two things – cravings and aversions. I see now that I am so helpless in front of all that controls us. Søren Kierkegaard once wrote in his journal, 'I feel as if I were a piece in a game of chess, when my opponent says of it, "That piece cannot be moved." So do I become a pawn when my sensations direct the course of my consumption of the world.' Until we realize this link between our urge to drink, eat, smoke, or do pretty much anything that we do, and the drive of our sensations to self-perpetuate, we won't be able to stop doing it, no matter how many nutritionists we visit, gyms we sign up for or counsellors we go to. We are directed by how we feel or how we want to feel. Meditation is the process of retraining the mind to not be quite so Pavlovian.

I would be lying if I said that after seven days, I don't feel hungry after the lunchtime meal. Or even tea. I do. I just don't feel the need to assuage that hunger. It is not life-threatening. It doesn't wake me up with the sounds of my stomach acids churning. I am not going to faint, because my body has the nutrition it needs. I am not diminished by my hunger, nor am I afraid of what it will do if it is left unattended. If it feels neglected, let it. If it feels upset, let it. That is not my feeling. That is a feeling I am conscious exists, but it is ceasing, bit by bit, to define me. I am not my hunger. I am not my thirst. Am I just torturing myself? Not really. I am still conscious of the fact that I can eat if I really want to. I'm pretty sure if I went to them and said I feel ill and really, really have to eat, they would give me something. I can still choose to leave and head straight to the nearest restaurant. I am not a prisoner here. I can go home and binge all day. I have booked myself into a five-star hotel in the plains for one night in order to be able to catch an early flight the morning after we leave here, but I already know I probably won't be attacking the breakfast spread these establishments typically have. The need to consume is diminished, but not eradicated. I don't think I will be able to eat dinner for a long while after this, if at all. In the course of my job, I work with a lot of nomadic tribes, and I have spent many hours with them in their homes and workplaces. I have always been saddened by the fact that no matter how prosperous they come to be in their small worlds, very few are even now able to afford more than one meal a day. It has bothered me immensely for years, and I do feel greedy when I overeat or when I have dinner. Of course, that's silly. The rockstar cannot better my position with his guilt any more than I can better that of others who have less than me. All I can do is write about it so the world knows, and maybe donate occasionally, but none of these are long-term fixes. We live in a world where increasingly more consumption, more of everything is the only answer we are providing for ourselves. More goods and services, more electricity, more water, more travel, more opportunity, more yield per acre, more, more, more. We are spinning in a vortex of more. To procure more, we and others who create that more, must do more. In this way, we are each reacting to each other's wants, tying each other into vortexes of need-generation. Perhaps at some point we can do with less. Minimalism, far from being a designer fad in a Parisian fashion house, derives from the Zen of this principle. Eat for hunger, consume to clothe, leave the rest. It is also a hallmark of the indigenous people everywhere. One of the articles I had done a while ago was about the difficulty a small cooperative bank in Ahmedabad was facing in teaching what saving meant to the nomads it wanted to extend credit to. For generations, they took what they needed and left the rest. They didn't have the concept of tomorrow. If the following day didn't offer them what they needed, they went without. I met the tribes during my travels and I thought of them now. How much trust and faith you must have in the world and its resources to surrender your tomorrows. All of society, all of life, tells us that this is the foolish way. When they tell us the story of the ant and the grasshopper, this is what they mean. Don't sing with abandon today when you ought to be foraging for winter. What you sowed yesterday, you will reap tomorrow. Sankharas are like that – our deeds, words and actions of yesterday will come to fruition tomorrow. Somehow, we fail to be completely oblivious to that natural progression. As with money or grain or any consumable, what we have sown yesterday will reap the harvest of our tomorrow, for better or for worse. The link is direct, clear and immediate. The less you sow, the less you react, the less you reap. All the minimalism of the Buddha is in this. Do not react. Do not sow. Do not reap. Just be.

I think about my son, his college, the fees, getting a job, savings... if something happens to me, will my insurance cover help him through his early life? We are all fraught with worry about ourselves and everything around us, because we imbue ourselves with a sense of responsibility and control. We imagine we have them. If my car tumbled off the mountainside and into the river on my way back, I think, that's it. There is no tomorrow, no matter how well-laid my plans may have been. There is only today. So perhaps all the things I have left pending for tomorrow – my manuscripts, my relocation to a small town where I can grow my own vegetables on a small piece of land, my savings and investments – need to happen today. Not tomorrow. Truth be told, I feel a little guilty thinking about material accumulations during the meditation sessions, but how can I not? Are we not each of us responsible for others? Some financially, others socially, morally? Does the fact of my meditation suddenly cut me loose from those responsibilities I shoulder?

In the Teacher's discourses, his wife, Elaichi Devi, is always seated next to him, though she doesn't speak. This is to show that he is not a monk, he is a householder. And dhamma is accessible to everyone, even the householder. I am not required to renounce my life in order to obtain liberation. It won't come after death. If it comes to me, it must come now, as I am, effective and apparent in what I do; only then is any awareness of the self useful and pragmatic. I must find more efficacious ways to be a better householder, one who acts with morality and correctness. A sage in the jungle who is angry at no one is not nearly as effective as the sage in the city who manages to control his temper, it is said. I wholeheartedly agree. If there is no one to provoke you, you can't really claim to be even-tempered. What helps instead is the refusal to take things personally. I feel like vipassana teaches me how to do this. It doesn't promise me that my provocateurs will magically be removed from my path, or that obstacles won't present themselves, that critics fair and unfair won't have their say. It is just that none of these things will matter. It may matter to others, but it won't matter to me. I am not obliged to react.

I am still not able to concentrate on my vipassana rounds for over forty-five minutes. I have begun to give up earlier and more periodically. I open my eyes every now and then. I tell myself it's okay to let it go for now, that I can try harder in the next session. This comes with the realization that I am going to be practising this for a long time to come. I don't feel the urge to see instantaneous results. Though, truth be told, I am worried that at home I will not have these multiple opportunities and these hours-long sessions to come to focus. At best, maybe between chores and work and family and rest, I will find an hour in the morning if I wake up early enough. I doubt I will wake by 4 a.m. there, though I am an early riser. The immediate aftermath of my waking hours is punctuated by the dog, the dog walker, the milkman, the garbage collector, the dog's food, checking my emails and messages, making some tea and catching up with the news.

This consumes an hour, and then I begin to write. Before I know it, it's broad daylight and there are people and tasks and duties zipping through my day on motorized wheels till it's time to stop. I will have to fix a slot, as I have heard the assistant teacher tell some old students repeatedly. Time management is of the essence – make the time.

The cold has aggravated my bronchitis, and I am breathing deeply and noisily every now and then. I foolishly try to focus my concentration on my breath to make it easier and have fewer interruptions. As I breathe deeply, I focus on my breath going in all the way to my diaphragm, feel the flow of the air and all the body parts it courses through. A few minutes of doing this, and the breath is now coinciding with my rounds. I feel someone pull at my cushion until I open my eyes. It is Dechen. The assistant teacher wants to see me. He looks irritated.

'Is this how you normally breathe?' he asks angrily. 'You are only supposed to focus on the regular breath. You are not supposed to create intentional breath. You are creating intentional breath for sustained periods of time. By now, your breathing should be irrelevant – your focus should be only on the body.' He is worried that I have wasted the course and have not got it right and, worse, that he is responsible for not correcting me earlier on. I consider what he is saying and decide to spare him the agony. 'Yes,' I say. 'What yes?' he asks. 'Yes, this is how I breathe.' It's technically not a lie because

I do breathe more deeply when I am in high altitudes due to my illness, which I had told him about earlier. Although even I know that I can take my focus off it and just let the normal breath flow too. So he is right, I am doing it wrong. I don't know if it is my ego at not wanting to be called out in front of the whole class, or just stubbornness, but I insist I am breathing this way because of my bronchitis and I cannot change it. He relaxes a little, realizing he has been harsh to judge me. 'Try and not regulate it so deeply,' he advises me. 'Otherwise your concentration will shift from the body and its sensations to the breath, and you will not get past it.'

I realize what he is saying is correct and for my benefit, so when I go back to my seat, I clamp down on the intentional breathing. It takes me a while to snap out of the rhythm, but in time it goes back to normal again and I have forgotten, like the centipede who began to count his legs as he marched and then forgot which foot to put in front of the other, if I am breathing one way or other.

Today the Teacher tells us to not just scan up and down, but also back to front, to explore the internal organs as well and the sensations we feel. I suspect my feeling the heaviness of my lungs is already a part of this scan, but I contemplate my tongue now. It has been still, but surely so much is said that cannot be unsaid, it must bear quite a burden through the lifetimes. I notice an itchy sensation every time I pass over it. Perhaps, I think, that's also from the things I am yet to say. I finish one round and leave the spinal cord for last. As I travel up and down its length, I see that it has clearly borne the brunt of all my pig-headedness for decades. Those of us the world likes to call strong are actually intensely fragile, and if it weren't for my spine, I would have collapsed a long time ago. I owe it so much. I spend a few minutes travelling its length with gratitude and contemplating its pain. It feels like a deep tissue massage. I get into my inner ears and all the burning things they must have heard over lifetimes. The most pain is still in my womb.

Jitnā gehrā rāag hai
utanā gehrā dveṣa;
jitnā gehrā dveṣa hai
utnā gehrā kleśa

Deeper the craving,
deeper the aversion;
deeper the aversion,
deeper the affliction.

So the evening verse goes. This is going to take a while, and I have come to feel a sense of patience, where once was resignation, about the pain I have to exorcize.

We have been walking around like popsicles all day, and I notice that Ana has only a single layer, a flannel sweatshirt, on. She is constantly rubbing her palms together. I hand her my gloves and stuff my fingers in my pocket. By evening, the clouds have returned and it is going to rain some more. The mountains have receded to where they came from.

We have only one more complete day of serious meditation. The day after, they will give us back our phones in the mid-morning session, they tell us. We will need to reconfirm our bookings and tickets, but this is also so that the outside world doesn't come as too much of a shock after so much isolation. It's to ease us in. I am uncomfortable, and actually find myself wishing I don't get my phone back. Only the thought of calling my son and apologizing to him with the new-found understanding of my own transgressions excites me. He should know, more than anyone else in the world, that he is a good person and that I am proud of him, that everything that he is is enough. Every day that I am unable to convey this is one day too much.

I notice that my snoring has disappeared. At least, I think it has. A new predilection has taken its place. For some strange reason, when I lie down, I feel myself tilting to the right. Maybe I spent too much time contemplating my right ear, I think, as sleep brings with it a rapidly descending cloud of oblivion. Aeschylus sounds in my ears as I drift off: 'Even in our sleep, pain which cannot forget falls drop by drop upon the heart until, in our own despair, against our will, comes wisdom through the awful grace of god…'

Day 9

Tilting at Windmills

I FEEL LIKE BY NOW I WAS MEANT TO BE ON A CLOUD surrounded by gorgeous golden peaches and hand-rolled chocolate on trays with the choicest wine poured from a silver jug into a crystal chalice, while being serenaded by an angel orchestra as God and I exchange notes on what my dream future should ideally be. But nope. The dementors are at my head and are sucking out my mind in wispy clouds, I kid you not. The nocturnal tilt now has me at a full-scale lean. I imagine I look like one of those Bajaj autorickshaws when a too-large gentleman sits on one side rather than in the middle, and the driver has to ask him to shift his weight or they won't be able to go. I am a ship with all the cargo in its hold pressing the leeward side a couple of inches into the water. I am the tower of Pisa just when the tilting began and they still believed they could set it right. You get the picture. When I walk from the room to the meditation hall and from there to the breakfast hall, I am at a slant. When I sit to meditate, I begin well enough, but within minutes, I find myself at a 45-degree angle to the ground and in a state that seems something between a light sleep and an engrossing daydream. I have no clue what this is. And here I was determined to have a great last day of meditation. I was to arise refreshed and splendid, a true seeker of the self. Instead, here I am, unable to even sit up straight. I am not sure at this point if anyone can see what I feel. Am I actually walking at an angle or is this in my head? While we have sneakily violated rules for some gesticulation and eye contact, I have no real way to have a full-fledged conversation yet, and so cannot ask if anyone else can see me tilt. Anyway, it's just one more day, so maybe I can ride it out, I think. I go take a bath and use some extra hot water to scrub the tilt out of me. I succumb to the Sikkimese way and wash my hair in this desperate cold, guarding my toes from any potential shower of icicles as I rub my mane dry.

I feel refreshed, and not in the least sleepy, but still angular. Maybe I have damaged my inner balance somehow, maybe this is the onset of spondylitis, or perhaps my bronchitis sent a cold into my inner ear or something, I tell myself, and make it a point to drink more hot water. The electricity goes out and the water in the dispenser remains tepid today. Just my luck. I try to take my mind off this strange sensation and focus on the verse for the day. It feels a little ironic.

Sukh āye nāce nahiṅ
Dukh āye nahiṅ roye
donoṅ meṅ samarasa rahein
toh hi maṅgal soye

Not dancing when pleasure comes,
not wailing when in pain,

keeping equilibrium in both –
this is the greatest welfare.

This focus on equilibrium feels like a practical joke right now. I smile wryly at the Teacher in my head. Good one, I tell him. Now, can I just sit up straight? I try making the request humbly again. No response. I can still feel myself being tugged at like my dog on a walk when he has decided he wants to go that way and I want to go this. It feels like I am pulling against a deep sleep to get back to my focus and meditative rounds. Worry sets in, and I realize I am up against something I don't understand. I open my eyes and decide to wait the session out. I try to do my rounds with my eyes open, but I catch the assistant teacher looking at me every time I do. So I have to alternate between keeping my eyes open and shut. This feels like a metaphor for my life somehow. I am immensely thankful when the lunch bell rings and I grab Dechen. She chuckles. 'Yes, it happens,' is all that she will offer. 'The vibrations in the hall are quite strong as it is an old centre, so the impact is greater.' Impact? What impact? Am I going to be pulled this way and that in meditation now? Sounds bizarre. My understanding is it is like the pulsing of the speakers again – I must pull my mind off it and focus on the body every time it happens. She asks if I want to ask the assistant teacher, but I don't want to be that kid in class who puts their hand up every time there is a question hour. Besides, what will I do from tomorrow, when we head home? I feel like the problem with ashram situations is that they encourage dependence on the teacher, on constant instruction, and cultivate a kind of unquestioning devotion. What I actually like about vipassana is that my discovery is all my own. Nobody decides for me whether I am a beginner or if I have advanced or not, even if they observe the signs. I want to explore the revelations my mind and body are handing me now. 'Nope, it's okay. I'll handle it,' I tell her. 'If it gets unmanageable, I will ask to see the assistant teacher.' Dechen nods. She understands. 'At some point, even teachers can't help. They can guide you based on their experience, but you have to travel the path yourself,' she says wisely, reading my mind. I contemplate the notion of whether self-sufficiency is also a kind of arrogance. It would be foolish not to ask for help when you really need it, I figure; after all, that is what a sangha is for. But to know when you really need it will come with self-awareness, I guess. At this kindergarten stage, we are still fearful and learning to walk. At some point, at least on Day 9, maybe I should let go of mom's finger.

I go back to my meditation, and the afternoon session is calmer and less about frantically making the most of the time we have left, which was the energy of the morning. It is muggy, drizzling all day, and while it is the full moon of Holi, it is unlikely that we will be able to glimpse it. Already the mood is less fraught. It's not a great success in terms of focus, and the hold the concentration has had over the mind is slipping. I do want to go home now, hug my son, have a bath in my own bathroom, get out of layers of clothing and sleep on my own bed.

I turn my focus to the chants of the day, which are an enumeration of the highest welfare by the Buddha. Asevana ca balanam, the avoidance of fools, is number one, and I ponder if the Buddha would be amenable to a high-five. I really like him. The list of what constitutes the highest welfare includes company of the wise, giving honour where it is due, suitable dwelling, learning, skill, serving parents, peaceful occupation, generosity, blameless deeds, shunning intoxicants and evil, vigilance in dhamma, humility, contentment and gratitude.

I am among the many who like to think of ourselves as essentially good. Sure, we've made mistakes, but we do not harm another intentionally. When we err, we seek to make amends. We stand by the things we have been taught are true. We don't rob, steal, kill. In principle, to me, this is good. The rest is honestly a bit nebulous. By these high moral codes, I pretty much have no hope of salvation any more. Where the Buddha and the Teacher have been telling me everything they are is accessible, I can see now that we're back at all the dos and don'ts that make this an impossible stretch. Forget all this, the five silas, do not kill, do not lie, I already know I'm going to eat fish at the very least when I return and I am probably going to tell a couple of white lies. To the boss, 'Hey, I was just going to call you …'; to a friend, 'Hey, no, am out of town that weekend. Sorry, can't make it …'; to family, 'Yeah, yeah, everything is fine …' So is there a point to what I am doing? Am I not beyond redemption? Is this not Yeats's turning and turning in the widening gyre? You said be real, say it as you see it, so I'm telling you, this is me. I don't know if I can be all these things. I know I'm not a bad person, but hell's bells, I'm no saint either, and unlikely to be one in the next couple of lifetimes. At this point, dear Teacher, look, I've crossed forty and I don't know if I can push myself to be all this. I'm just about getting comfortable with my blurred boundaries, if you know what I mean. The Teacher keeps saying what he has to say. We're not meeting in the middle. I guess I'm on my own on this one.

The Teacher speaks of how the ego arises because we have this self-image to maintain. It's what we think ourselves to be and what we want others to think of us. When something shows us to be other than what we perceive ourselves to be, we say we are harmed. I would like to be thought of as capable, efficient, and when a colleague describes someone I am not, I think they are out to get me. To me, this person then is petty and harmful. We believe someone to be evil, but if we think about it, they are not evil to their relatives or their friends, or to their social circuit. From other angles, to other people, they are genuinely loved and cared for. So people come and tell us,

'Oh, no, you must be mistaken, I know that guy, he is really nice.' Yes, but he wasn't nice to me, was he? I have to come to the understanding that my perception of reality is not the only perception there is. My view of a situation or a person is not the absolute word on that situation or that person. Other views, other perspectives exist. I also do not bother to investigate why I seem that way to that person. Whether I can change anything I am doing to alter that perception. I am focused on changing him, his speech, his environment, his control over his perception and the way other people respond to it. Those things are not in my control. The only thing that is in my control is the way I react to him, or the action I perform that creates that reaction in him.

The danger when we box and label people in this way, good and bad, evil and angel, is that we are concretizing our fragmented version of the truth. We believe our version of the truth to be absolute. When the person does something not aligned with what we have put in our box, we say they have disappointed us or surprised us.

Think about it as directed towards yourself. I know people who behave with some surprise that I have accomplished something I always knew I could. 'Oh, we didn't believe you actually would,' they say, and it irritates me. Tomorrow, when I emerge from the course, my siblings will laugh and say, 'Hey, we expected you to exit by Day 5,' and rib me about not being able to stay silent for so long. I laugh, but it irks me. Because it presumes to know me, and nobody does. None of us know each other. Not really. We barely know ourselves. Yet, here we all are, casting these judgements on others, believing the versions of them that we know to be the only versions there are. To release these images, of ourselves as well as others, makes our passage through life so much easier.

As the Teacher describes this, I think about my son. Because I have brought him up, I expect that I know him. I think it is an insult to me and my parenting skills to suggest that I don't know him through and through. Yet, he will grow, and learn, and become, regardless of me. Because he is his own person who absorbs influences and carries his own karma and baggage and sankharas across his own lifetimes. He has his own chain of actions and reactions to disentangle from. He has the influence of his friends, his extended family. His experiences and ways of processing his own life. I am, I realize now, just a part of that complex kaleidoscopic whole. Who am I to presume to know, to judge, to contain?

When we are told that a person we love has hit someone, or wounded someone, or harmed someone, we immediately assume to know them best, and claim there is no way they would have done so. We don't like to think about the people we love as capable of the negative. That comes from loyalty, belonging, ownership, but also from presumption. We constantly react to our imagined perception of the person and rarely see who they are in their entirety. When we tell our kids, 'You didn't appear for this competitive examination like I wanted you to, and I am disappointed in you,' our disappointment has not been caused by them. It has been caused by our creation of the expectation that they would be aligned with what we perceive them to be. 'I wanted to see you go be an engineer, but you wanted to be a DJ,' (or, in my case, the opposite actually – I would like my son to be in a creative field and he wants to be a lawyer) is a statement of our expectation and our disappointment, not theirs. They didn't disappoint us, or anyone. You or I disappointed ourselves. It's a small but relevant gap in perception. It becomes the root of all our disappointments, this inability to see people as they are, rather than as we imagine them to be. We then shower them with our disappointment, and rue that somewhere the relationship went awry. It didn't. What we sowed, we reaped.

A few years hence, my son will be in his own romantic relationships and be a person I don't know today. I trust that he will be a gentleman, kind, considerate and sure-footed, but he will also be romantic and needy, passionate and argumentative in ways that I cannot contemplate. I know now with certainty, no matter how much of a chill mom I think I am or have been, I have to release this mental labelling and boxing, and allow him to be his own person to completion. In the teenage years, this is the gap between children and parents that doesn't get bridged, because we think we know them, and own that knowledge, instead of releasing it with acceptance and interrupting it with our own perspective of the truth. I have to give him the space to be his own person, mistakes, passions and all. Realizing this is the biggest outcome of this exercise I have undertaken. The sankhara is sown with the reaction to a false perception or expectation one has of others. When I see this, I see that there is no blame to be heaped on others. For anything at all, past or present or future. It's all me…

The post-lunch session is languorous, with a dull, grey sky. It is the second last day of our stay, and I have no clue why people are still washing their clothes and hanging them out to dry. Perhaps it gives them something to do. Perhaps they are just meticulous. I grab a chair and risk climbing a little way up the mountainside where there is a small flat ledge just right for the view. In my first attempt to climb it holding the chair with one hand, I slip down the gravelly hillside and land on my bum. I petulantly try again and make it this time. The perch of the chair is rocky and unstable. Still, I take to it like I have conquered my own little Everest. I hope I don't have to get up to pee or it doesn't start raining now, because I'm going to look quite foolish. Sita passes by and waves to me, and gesticulates at her leg. She has never attempted to communicate with me before, so I just smile back, glad that the communication is increasing as we approach the end. She tries again and I smile back, concerned at her concern. I think she means the chair is not stable on its perch. I wiggle it to reassure her it's sitting well. She laughs and turns away. I focus my attention on the mountains again; this time I want to see if I can make out the outlines of the Kanchenjunga ridge behind the cloud cover. In a few minutes, Sita returns excitedly jabbering to Dechen. Dechen bursts into peals of laughter. Sita is trying to tell me leeches are about to start climbing up my leg, Dechen informs me. I am out of the chair and sliding back down to the ground before you can say Kanchenjunga. Dechen and Sita go off laughing, Ana is guffawing, Neena wryly smiling, and I spot Raima, who sometimes stands in the pathway and gazes upon her home in Gangtok, hide a grin. Maybe sometimes it is good to react.

My tug of war with the dementors continues through the day. Sometimes I give in and fall into whatever somnolence they slip me into, which is surprising because I have never slept during a meditation session so far. Other times, I win and regain my concentration, even if only fleetingly. But it is exhausting. So far, I was only working towards something. Now, I am working against something too.

'If you can't use vipassana every day,' the Teacher says that night, 'then it just becomes another rite or ritual or meaningless ceremony.' Self-help techniques teach you to count to ten, drink water, distract yourself when you need to cool down, not say something you'll only regret, but such techniques don't actually remove your negative reaction; they just suppress it. If you're in a really bad situation, that's just going to build up over time and explode when you least need it to. Another technique is to vent your rage, speak your hurt, but that will have its ripple reactions too. The middle path is to neither deny nor acknowledge, but to simply observe. All very well to say, but how do you observe something as abstract as a reaction? There are two ways: One is to observe the physical sensation it leaves in the body, that little burn in the pit of the stomach, that resentment held in a tight ball in the chest. Secondly, observe how your breath changes in intensity. When you're angry or agitated, you start breathing faster, when you're calm, you're generally breathing slowly and without any audible sound, nor does your body respond with upheaval. Where earlier, reaction was instantaneous, now, it is prefaced by this observation. 'What is my body gathering up to say?' you are asking yourself. So you could pre-empt the negativity by staying silent or cutting off harsh words, or removing yourself from an emotional response rather than simply responding in the moment. The Teacher calls this pause the shock absorber.

To be totally realized, you need to have ten paramis in your kitty. These are mental qualities. Nekkhamma, renunciation; sila, morality; viriya, effort; panna, wisdom; khanti, tolerance; sacca, truth; adhitthana, strong determination; metta, pure selfless love; upekkha, equanimity; and dana, charity. As you can tell, I am way up there on the path to sainthood. I won't lie, at some point during this, my heart sinks a little at the prospect of all these impossible things to be. My bucket list simply has: visit Kyoto, Prague, Dubrovnik; find a good travel companion; write an award-winning novel; lose weight – all of which, I presume, are in there to feed my ego, add to my wants and inflate my bank balance. I try to look out of the blacked-out window and think about my life outside. Maybe I'll never be a monkish person. I like buying saris too much. I love to cook and share meals with friends. I do love life – immensely. Perhaps I won't ever have a halo around my head and have people show up at my funeral spouting eulogies of how much I had transformed and contributed to their lives. I doubt they will name library wings after me, or streets, or build statues in my memory. But hey, I won't ever spark a war or armed conflict. And my friends and family will always know they are loved and welcome, as will any rescue dog or cat that comes my way. I have plenty. And the good life is about appreciating and valuing what is, not chasing after or finding someone to blame for what isn't, right? I'm good.

I go to bed today, still tilting in ways that are so definitely not all my fault, knowing that I am good.

Day 10

Sweet Release

IMAGINE THAT YOU HAVE BEEN INVITED TO THE Great Indian Wedding, and the parents of the bride and the groom insist you eat to your heart's content before you leave. Even though you are not very hungry, since they are serving you delicacies with their own hands and looking after you like you were their very own, you can't really say no. When you reach the threshold of near-explosion and you have to insist on getting up from your seat at the table, it is spontaneous, written in some secret cultural scripture somewhere, that a blessing rises from within your very full stomach and overflows into the atmosphere, settling on the happy couple. It is an old Indian trick to accumulate good wishes, as any grandmother knows. Metta bhavana is the spiritual equivalent. You have meditated so much that your heart overflows with spontaneous goodwill in pretty much the same way.

The Teacher is using his Amitabh Bachchan baritone again, which is how I know he is sending a serious blessing our way and setting the vibrational temperature of the room. His voice is hypnotic as he chants the ten verses that constitute good feelings towards all. In translation, it only means one thing that he has repeated many times before: may all beings be happy. He emphasizes it with all kinds of beings – related, unrelated, teachers, friends, family, relatives, children – in all kinds of directions. May all we have encountered, and those we haven't, be suffused with good luck, goodwill, positive energy, success and prosperity. May they partake of whatever merits we have earned. May they want to seek dhamma too. May they suffer no grief, no pain. May they find ways to be relieved of their suffering. By the time he finishes, the room is pulsing with positive energy so loud that you can hear the low hum of its vibration. It's like resetting your Wi-Fi connection. Now you are tuned in at a whole different frequency and can access that which vibrates with you – the compassion is tangible.

Love is so distinctly different from compassion, it is made apparent. Love is selfish. It wants, it owns, it seeks. It also distinguishes. We love some, we hate others. It is invested in outcomes. When we love, we expect certain behaviours, no matter what Shakespeare says. Compassion puts some distance between you and the object of compassion. It is not personal. You can't hurt me by not accepting my compassion. It flows towards you regardless. But don't take it personally either; it flows in pretty much the same quality and quantity towards an earwig or an owl.

The goodwill we wish upon others exists in all philosophies. In Hinduism it is the simple 'Loka samasta sukhino bhavantu' repeated three times, so that all the beings of the three worlds are happy. But we rarely define what that happiness means. Here, it is to ask that others share our merit and our learnings, their outcomes and benefits.

It is a reminder that even as we untie the knots we tie ourselves into, our progress is inextricably tied to the cycle of action and reaction we engage in with others. A butterfly that flaps its wings does change the world. We are all doing so much more than just that. If we wish progress, spiritual or material, only for ourselves, we cannot progress as a larger sangha. We will each be an obstacle to the other, because we are constantly bouncing our reactions off each other. Hostility for hostility, want for want, longing for longing. We are the end to each other's anger, pride, hate, lust, greed. One of us has to walk away. This time, let it be me. So I don't get saddled with that all the time, I must also wish that you arrive at that conclusion too. From the next time, it will also be you walking away. That is the non-reactiveness multiplied. We can only benefit, especially in times like these, in a world that constantly seems to be in defensive mode, everyone gearing up to take offence at the other.

All that is mutates in time, the good as much as the bad. Our reactions set off outcomes that linger long after the original circumstance has passed. Its impact is always on people. Inasmuch as we are all aspirants, sadhakas, alone, we are nothing without the sangha, each other. We have the potential to bring each other down, interrupt each other's practices by our reactions, as much as we have the potential to boost each other up. That goes as much for the little sangha that we are each a part of now, as for our extended social circuits back home.

The Teacher asks for just one thing, which will remind me to continue my practice in the days to come, even when I don't feel like meditating much. He asks for dakshina, the Teacher's fee, which is for us to send metta bhavana out to him and to others every day. I make a mental note to do this as often as I can, because I am truly grateful for what I have learnt here.

They give us our phones shortly after, and I switch it on to ignore 1,065 emails and a message from my son saying he is off on a picnic with his friends and might not be reachable. I'd like to tell you I was calm, but at one point, everyone around me came to ask why I was looking so agitated. I tried to contact him several times, but he didn't pick up. Finally he called back a couple of hours later. He was ill and had skipped the picnic. As my mind flooded with relief, I decided I couldn't wait any more.

I told him what I had learnt of myself and my reactiveness, and apologized to him for all the times I had overreacted. It was not his fault – none of it was. Sure, he could stand to pick up his towel and put his clothes in the laundry basket every now and then, but that's the worst of him. He's a gem of a kid, and I told him I needed him to know that before he stepped out in the world. It couldn't wait a moment longer. He broke down and cried. It didn't matter, he said, because he knew everything I had been through and when sometimes he couldn't understand why I was so angry or upset, he told himself it was coming from somewhere else, a transference of everything that others had done to me, and he let it go. He shouldn't have had to be so mature, so understanding, that was my job, I told him. There are no others and there is no blame. There is just me taking responsibility for my actions and reactions. I need to let things go and he has been a little Solomon, wiser than everything that I came here to discover about myself. 'That's okay, mom,' he said. 'We're a team.' Then I cried too. My sangha gathered around me to ask if I was okay. In that moment, I knew that as much as I had been dreading his leaving home and my own future post that, he would be good wherever he went, and I would be good too.

Be happy,
be happy!

Mana-mānasa mein pyār hi
urmila urmila hoye
roma-roma se divan uthe
mangala mangala hoye

May rapture spread
through the pool of the mind.
May every pore give forth the sound,
be happy, be happy!

That evening there is a hailstorm and we chatter like birds on a perch, taking shelter from the golf ball–sized pellets as they thunder down from the skies. We've taken selfies, exchanged phone numbers and made a WhatsApp group of our own on which we vow to meditate together virtually and stay in touch. We ask each other if we're okay and whether we've come to decisions about our lives, families and relocation plans. We have bonded in ways that I never knew were possible in the complete silence of adults who are essentially strangers. We have seen each other break down and face our worst fears together, and we have acquired a healthy respect for each other's tribulations. We know none of our lives, no matter how privileged we may seem, have been easy. My roomie asks me my name finally. I can finally tell her she snores too. We laugh. We are not supposed to touch each other, but I'm pretty sure there was some hugging. We run down to the office to make our donations, buy books and catch up with the officials. We discover the food is so excellent here in this centre because the cook joins us for meditation sessions too, and the administrators believe his good vibes energize the food he makes. We thank him profusely. I run into the assistant teacher and tell him I have a question. Jessica has one too. He asks us to come to the hall at noon.

She goes first and to my surprise, she's asking the same question I have. She feels a pull and a tilt too. I wonder if it is because we touched each other, which we were not supposed to do. I don't mention it; it's too late to resolve anyway. The assistant teacher gives her the same answer he will give me shortly. It is Mara, the negative forces the Teacher mentions that try to pull your attention away from the positive. It is at best a distraction that you simply have to pull your mind away from and overcome. 'Don't worry,' he says. 'Its pull won't be so strong once you leave here, because the vibrations are stronger here.' Like a cell phone closest to the tower, we are receiving both the positive and the negative at full strength. Oh, goodie! I get to go home with my own personal dementor, I think. I try not to add to the heebie-jeebies it gives me. I wonder if I am going to be pulled into the netherworld where my mind will be locked into a dungeon somewhere while my body lies in a coma here, but quickly pull myself back from being consumed by the negative. I get back to catching up. The biggest dementor this dementor hasn't encountered yet is the cell phone. There are hotels and flights and taxis to confirm, and relatives to inform that we are back from *Into the Wild*.

I try to concentrate, but by evening, we're already one foot in another world. I will come back to this form of meditation I know, I hope. But I have also learnt to allow my mind its effervescence, like freshly shaken soda. As the taxi pulls away the next morning, and we separate to go our different ways, we may meet again or we may not. That is broadly irrelevant to the sangha. We have known ourselves in the presence of each other and there is no revelation quite like that. There is trust, there is respect, there is peace, there is harmony, there is communion. With ourselves as much as with others. Which is all one needs anyway.

Epilogue

THE FARTHER YOU MOVE FROM THE CELL PHONE TOWER, the weaker your signal becomes. Then, one day, in the middle of the conversation, you are shouting, 'Hello? Hello? Can you hear me?' into the phone, as though you are your great-aunt Sushila who has suddenly gone hard of hearing. Except, a month down the line, this is you, talking to yourself. You have meditated, even followed the new limited eating schedule for a week – okay, maybe even a fortnight. You find yourself clearer in the head, less impulsive, more prone to considered thought. You watch your emotions more. You are not less provoked to anger; things and events still irritate you, but you are less reactive. You find yourself simply disregarding the impulse to show them what's what. Then, one day, you skip a scheduled meditation slot, and then another. Over time, the WhatsApp sangha dissipates, each lost to their own preoccupations, and they stop posting the meditating woman emoji and the time they are each meditating. Friends and relatives stop being enthralled by your experience. You are alone in your spiritual practice again. You and your mind, its ruts, your habits – old friends on a lonely path. You have been consumed now by your responsibilities, duties and pleasures. Old patterns suck you in. You have begun eating those heavy dinners again. You go out for a drink with friends. You feel a twinge when you consume intoxicants and meats, but you swallow quickly and remind yourself that those rules only apply when you are actually in the course. You ignore the urge to remain suspended in the meditative state, as though you are a news anchor muting a pesky troll on social media that has said something so rude but so true that it hits home.

Occasionally, the Teacher's oft-repeated phrase, 'Break the habit pattern of the mind', flashes through, but here you are, firmly in the grip of the old pattern of the mind – Abhimanyu in the chakravyuh. You have taken to meditating once a week, which quickly becomes only now and then, when your memory catches a whisper of what it was like to feel centred. This is why the rigours of the ten-day course help. As with childbirth, our minds have a way of subduing the pain and offering up in hindsight the wholesomeness that emerged from a dulled agony. Exceptional moments of lucidity here and there, those rare breakthroughs into a singular alignment with oneself, rise above the tedium.

Transitory as even these have been, they linger – absolute shining orbs of pure bliss. Bubbles of perfection cocooning your body and mind. Evanescent as their existence may be, they find the strength to throw open a window to a view that will catch your breath, just when you are close to forgetting that such sublimity was ever possible. As you are rushing around completing a deadline, dealing with an irate boss, managing money, scolding your children, tiptoeing around a moody spouse, binge-eating with guilt, grumbling at the commute, on the precipice of despair, it floats suddenly through you, with you, ascending ever so gently to a higher plane where it diffuses into the ether. A tease of what was. A hint of who you momentarily were. An embryo of what it is possible to be birthed as again. A force so lucent as to encompass everything you are and do in that moment, gone, but leaving you instantly altered.

I nurse the urge to return. I will find myself back in two months, this time for a shorter four-day course in Igatpuri, the epicentre of vipassana teaching in India. This campus, spotted with offices and office-bearers, is vast, at a slight elevation, cool breezes wafting through the branches, mongooses running from bush to shrub and mynahs singing in the sprawling banyan trees, planted to design over forty years ago. My assistant teacher this time is a septuagenarian, lungi-wearing Jewish man from New York, who sits in ardhapadmasana with the agility of a teen monk.

From the moment I sit down at the first session, I feel the neglected pain course through my body with welcome. Where were you? they complain in a burst of pins and needles and deep aches. I apologize and embrace them in return. The meditation, a refresher for old students who have lost their practice, takes you back to the beginning. I am not so far gone that I need initiation again, but I find my mind disobeying the instructions to begin with ana-pana and instead rushing into vipassana. I pull it back, scold its hubris and reset it repeatedly. Ana-pana is the scalpel I need for the follow-up surgery. Ego, unresolved grudges, forgotten episodes, regrets and blame all rise up again. Yet, I notice, this time there is no all-consuming anger or overwhelming sorrow. My body is still, my tears are done, resolution is distinct; I am past so much and on the course to healing. The pain I feel now doesn't have me asking, 'Why? Why me?' any more. It is already distant, located in a limb here, a muscle there, disowned and disaffected, robbed of its power.

I instantly feel more familiarity with these sessions in the second course. We know what to do, we are given the leeway of seniors now. Some of us are more experienced than others. I am still flighty; my left leg catches a muscle pull and I am constantly moving to alleviate the pain. I am clearly kidding myself that I have acquired some stillness. There probably cannot be inward stillness if you are still noticeably outwardly restless. I notice the woman in front of me holds her position like carved marble through months of practice, and I aspire to that. Not on this trip, clearly, but okay, someday. Yet, it is evident what continued practice instils. A face shines, a posture sustains, a concentration holds, a serenity prevails, and these are just the apparent outward manifestations of the inner work. Telltale testimony of continued engagement. There is nobody to fool here but oneself. We each are assigned our own rooms and we are not monitored through every stage of the course. Sometimes, in the non-group sessions we go back to our rooms to meditate. There is little banter at the start of the course and we slip easily into our silences, even before stipulated.

Unlike many courses, vipassana doesn't coax you to keep coming back and take another course. There is no test of loyalty or growth except your own inner path. If it's working, you will know. If you are not progressing by way of your daily routine, taking every course in the system is not going to help you. The assistant teachers repeat this often. There are no tests for you to take, no one to impress with your progress, no hierarchy to fit into. It's just you and your mind.

I have a question during the Q&A session with the assistant teacher, but there are fewer questions now from any of us. When at home, I meditate better when I have the recording of the guided meditation playing. When I attempt an hour's meditation without it, my mind wanders and I manage about twenty-five minutes. Isn't this cultivating dependence? How is it different from relying on a mantra or a religious ritual? Isn't vipassana about moving beyond these?

The assistant teacher is precise and measured in his response. The goal of vipassana is to always move away from dependence. Even so, like a child who needs to go to the toilet and the mother who turns on the tap to help him, so too, my assistant teacher says, 'Be a mother to yourself. Help yourself along.' Compassion for oneself is the answer to many questions. I am stunned by the reminder that I too am deserving and in need of my own benevolence.

I have been hard on myself, expecting results like an exacting schoolmaster. Why am I in such a rush? My aim should not be to arrive anywhere quickly, but to acquire knowledge of myself surely. Submitting to the process is very different from seeking control over it. We seek mastery in these practices, forgetting that mastery is also a form of control. It speaks to our 'success' or 'failure' when there is really no such thing. There is just dawning awareness.

I return to my meditation with an understanding that I am here, in this state of inwardness, for as long as it takes. The process of understanding oneself is not a linear movement from point A to point B. It is an evolution of belonging from oneself to oneself. For those of us who have been fragmented, returning to wholeness is only possible through a compassionate embrace that gathers our smallest pieces. There's no line on the screen that tells you what percentage has been uploaded or charged. We are so used to looking to quantify progress, we forget that a genuine measure is not how many followers or likes or retweets we have. It is how encompassing the stillness is. And if you are genuinely enveloped in stillness, you are in the core of an unquantifiable space and an immeasurable time that is the now. There is no measure of the now. There is nothing ahead of the now. There is nothing behind the now. The now is. We are. I am. This is all. Nothing else matters.

How long has it been since nothing else mattered to you?

My breath pulses like a MacBook in sleep mode. The rising and falling of consciousness in rhythm with the buzz of the mosquitoes here. The assistant teacher has switched off the fan in the twilight session. It feels like a test of non-reactivity. Sweat pours down my face, but I do not make a move to wipe it. I watch it. I sense it. I acknowledge it. I feel incredible strength in conquering my sweat, the itch on my right forearm, the twinge in my left ankle. I cannot describe it any other way, this ability to not move when every impulse is screaming at you to. To defy yourself is an empowerment that leaves defying others or anything external redundant. When nothing has the power to move you, you have soaked up all the power in the room. All time, all energy, all movement, all impulse, all provocation, in that instant, ceases.

Since my return from Sikkim, even as my moments of awareness have faded, a clarity that hasn't existed before has settled in permanently. I feel its impact in two ways. One is I feel a distinct certainty in the decisions I make. The other is I feel no fear or doubt. Sometimes I wonder if this is just arrogance and folly. But even that categorizes itself as self-doubt and falls away. Arguments reduce, relationships heal. People I didn't really care about move away with reduced time and energy, and it doesn't matter. New relationships are forged. I have arrived at knowing where I want to move to and why. I make a trip down to Pondicherry with cousins and siblings to view a house owned by an artist that has come up for sale. I meet the architect instead and ask him to craft a simpler, more earthy home for me. I realize I have been following a career trajectory simply because I was on the route. I call it a day at my job, though incredulous friends and siblings ask me to reconsider, and think about what I really want to do. Many times people ask you, 'If money was no object, what would you do?' The question I ask myself now is: what would I do if I was not merely reacting to everything that had gone before? Each career move, the next job, is a link in a chain reaction to a previous one, linking back to a decision or a misconception dating back to when I was a teenager. What would I do if this moment was given to me anew? Who was I poised to become, that is the sum of me, in this living breathing moment? When you are honest with yourself, when the clutter falls away, when clarity cuts through the expectations you hold of yourself and that others hold of you, the answer comes quite simply.

I am a failure.

I do not say this with regret or anger, disappointment or self-loathing. I say it as someone who is not in a state of being what I have always wanted to be, a Ruth Prawer Jhabvala. I wanted to be a mother with many children, dogs, a large house, a garden, a view, an excellent cook, hosting friends around a large kitchen table, a self-sustaining farmer and a novelist. As people urge me to consider the prime location of my current home, near two major malls, a top school, a critical care hospital, and supermarkets, I see the value of these fading for me. I must admit I have given up on myself in the last decade or so, and have become that person who numbly resigns to fate. I look around and know I am not done. I don't see myself dying in the closed walls of a small room in the city. I want hills and sky, flowers and long walks. I want community and healing. Dogs, family, a stitched-together family. I want work that soothes. I want to give more of myself. All around, I want more.

Failure that I may be, I am still here. I have had to adapt and shift my goals. I smile, I live, I breathe, I feel pain, I seek joy, I defy definition, I walk my path, I find courage when I need it, I accept rejection, I embrace myself, I try again. No matter how many times I fail, I love repeatedly, bounteously, deeply. I express, I listen, I forgive, both myself and others. I read, I learn, I try. I believe. A well-honed survival instinct has pushed me to find detours when up against obstacles and antagonists. I know now I haven't listened to myself or the path. When you keep coming up against obstacles, the path itself is redirecting you elsewhere. But in our ingrained belief that we must fight against the world to succeed, we fail to listen to the obstacles or hear the pain. Failure also brings its own message. It is the redirection of energies better spent elsewhere. A lifetime of fighting to occupy places, claim titles, benefits, rights on paths I never even wanted to walk to begin with, can be exhausting. I am learning to value my own energy, and conserve it for myself, put it to better use, fill myself up. I have always been apart from my circumstances, apart from the litany of wrong turns, alive and vital.

In this moment, I see that this is also a gift. How do we live beyond our failures? How do we define ourselves apart from them? How do we embrace our pain? How do we heal? In this moment, I decide to retrain myself as a counsellor, but one who uses the inwardness of meditation to heal. It will be the beginning of a life-changing journey. In two months, unbeknownst to me at the time, I will return to college. I don't know how I will make a living in the days to come, but I know I am not afraid. In three months, I will be interning with cancer patients at the Tata Memorial Hospital. In four, with primary children at a local school. In six months, and then a year, my life will take inconceivable turns. One more year-ending short vipassana course down the line, I will accept a seat in a coveted master's dual-degree programme in counselling at New York University, scheduled to start in September 2020. In the meantime, I will set up Shamah, my mind+body+spirit counselling practice. I will conduct meditative walks for stressed-out women, form a support group for people grappling with urban isolation, conduct sessions to help people rebuild their lives as the coronavirus ravages their jobs, incomes, resources, health. As things crumble around me, I will find that the inner habit of cultivated equanimity kicks in to bolster me. Worried classmates, family, friends will call to ask: 'How are you not concerned?' 'What will happen now?' 'How will you study and earn?' 'Will all your plans be upended?' I will realize I don't have any more answers than they do, but what I do have is the lack of an urgency to know. I dwell in the unfolding; I ride the wave. I am able to respond to what is given or what is taken away with humour and the knowledge that this too will pass. I do what I can do, I release what I cannot. As I bail friends and clients out of the prisons of their anxiety, I will realize just how much the year and a half of meditation and therapy prepared me to deal with the impending uncertainty – not just for myself, but for others too. Sure, I send out inquiries for jobs and recommendations and gigs like everyone else, but an ease radiates from me, from a seemingly endless reserve. Nothing is life and death any more, not even imminent probable death. The virality of Covid-19 seems to me a simple physical manifestation of our deep interconnectedness. As the world confronts its mortality, I take to reading works like *Bardo Thodol*, the Tibetan Book of the Dead, translated by Robert Thurman, and the Dalai Lama and Desmond Tutu's *The Book of Joy*, and starting a podcast to reach out to more who need to hear words like these. The reading, the reaching out, the tele-counselling – the more that goes out from me the more it brings back to me in waves and I am constantly uplifted. The more I am isolated in quarantine, the more I seem to be connected. I witness for myself the difference between a reactive path and a responsive one as it unfolds in real time.

It will awe me how things fall into place, how the past ties its loose ends together unbidden, unfulfilled dreams from over twenty years ago stepping up to completion, how future fears dissolve in the certain steps of the now. Through all of them, I will feel the dissipation of myself in body and mind in the service of others, a metta bhavana that begins now.

On the final day of the four-day course, the Teacher administers the final metta bhavana. His voice seems deeper than usual, or perhaps I am better attuned to it. As he chants in Pali, I feel myself dissolve into the ether – the body and mind melting away into minuscule vibrations of compassion as I am carried with the wind into the far parts of the earth, free to be consumed as a microcosm of energy by anyone who needs it. I feel intrinsically linked to the pain and joy of those around me, and yet, disaffected.

I understand universality in a way I never have before. I understand what it is to come home.

Acknowledgements

I have come to understand that this book is scripting my life more than I it. I thank S.N. Goenka, for his vision and meticulous organization. My teachers, Amal Ghosh and Daniel Mayer, for lending me the guidance of their years of practice. The administrators of Dhamma Sikkim, Dhamma Vipula and the Vipassana Institute at Igatpuri for their voluntary service and the opportunity they continue to provide seekers like me. Gratitude to the various members of my sangha for providing me a continuing support system I didn't know I lacked.

To my parents, Laxmi and Jayaraman, for being open-minded seekers and voracious readers themselves; my brother, Gautam, for his steady emotional and financial backing and his lived equanimity; and my sister, Gauri, for her constant enthusiasm and spirit. To my son and teammate, Dhruv, for his keen analysis and arguments erring on the side of reason and atheism. The world needs more like you.

This book wouldn't have seen the light of day without the faith of my agent, Kanishka Gupta, which met the embrace of my publisher, Poulomi Chatterjee, who along with my commissioning editor, Rukmini Chawla Kumar, took a chance on an unusual piece of writing. This book had its quirks and unique character polished in the skilled hands of my editor, Cibani Premkumar, whose attention took it beyond what even I thought it could be. The illustrations you see here are the immense talent of Anwesha Ganguly, because of which this book catches the light as you turn the pages. I owe Aditi Nichani and the marketing team at Hachette cake and ale for aligning their strength behind it and powering its impact so keenly.

I also thank Zitto for the benevolence of paws on the keyboard that did not delete the whole manuscript before it could make it to the other side.